A Girl Named Betsy

A Girl
Named
Betsy

Betsy Burch

ARCHWAY
PUBLISHING

Archway Publishing books may be ordered through booksellers or by contacting:

Archway Publishing
1663 Liberty Drive
Bloomington, IN 47403
www.archwaypublishing.com
1 (888) 242-5904

Because of the dynamic nature of the Internet, any web addresses or links contained in this book may have changed since publication and may no longer be valid. The views expressed in this work are solely those of the author and do not necessarily reflect the views of the publisher, and the publisher hereby disclaims any responsibility for them.

Any people depicted in stock imagery provided by Thinkstock are models, and such images are being used for illustrative purposes only. Certain stock imagery © Thinkstock.

ISBN: 978-1-4808-4272-4 (sc)
ISBN: 978-1-4808-4273-1 (hc)
ISBN: 978-1-4808-4274-8 (e)

Library of Congress Control Number: 2017904191

Print information available on the last page.

Archway Publishing rev. date: 4/25/2017

To Mom

Acknowledgments

I want to say thank you for the love and support to the following people in my life. Without them, this book would not be possible: First and foremost, the wonderful love of my mother; who always believed in me and encouraged me to be independent and courageous. My Aunt Adele and Gran, whose unconditional love for me will never be forgotten. My writing coach, Nanda Olney, who spent hours looking over picture albums and journals of poster child years and helped me put my story together.

My shaman, energy healer, and life coach, Tracy Liebmann. For in this journey, you helped me discover my light and my truth. My best friends, Gillian Leaphart and Jill Cleary. My forever friend Steven Petersen. Your friendship has always and will always mean the world to me. My Inspiration, Nancy Burpee, who I admire and love dearly. Thank you for your encouragement in the sport of swimming. My husband Eric Stinnett. My prosthetist, Steven Kramer, and the wonderful staff of Carolina Orthotics and Prosthetics. Kevin Maurice with Kevin Maurice Photography and Cathy Snider with LeNor photography. My siblings, Sara and John. Sheila Foster and those in my life I hold most dear.

In loving memory of Nancy Olsen Lynch.

Contents

Preface

What's in a story anyway? I feel many things are: love, hate, hope, discouragement, defeat, and triumph. Things we can all relate to because, as humans, we all have experienced them. We are often told life is a journey. But what exactly does that mean? And if life is a journey, does that make the pain of life any easier? I think it can. Life can be painful—heartbreaking, in fact. However, it can be most beautiful and enlightening. Life is a journey indeed, but through the years, I learned part of that statement is missing. Life is a journey, and it can be a good one if you so desire and intend it to be. Our intentions and our energy, ever flowing and changing, positive and negative, are what we manifest into our lives.

This book moves between present day and the past. My hope is that as others read my story, they will reminisce their own past to see how life has been manifested into the present and perhaps find ways to enlighten the future. We all have stories. Understanding our personal journeys, I believe, can help us become enlightened for the future.

Excerpt below taken from my blog, Strong Amputee (strongamputee.com), the day after I completed the 10K bridge run:

It was amazing ... I captured the moments as I was nearing the finish line and put them in my playback memory box in my mind. People were "high five-ing" me, telling me to keep going ... keep going. Not to mention throughout the 10K, people would pass me and say "You are an inspiration"; - not to mention the thumbs up, so many I lost count. All these things reaffirm my belief that people are good.

I needed these motivating gestures as I was on the last mile. To be honest, at one point during the last mile, I felt like I was going to be sick. I kept telling myself: deep breaths deep breaths. I know it was only a 10K, but I felt I was starting to "hit the wall" or "the bonk"; when runners are almost completely depleted of the glycogen stores in their body. My muscles ached, my ankle and foot were throbbing, and my stomach was turning. I could just picture the lactic acid party my muscles were having; but I did get across the finish line and I was in a state of euphoria. I didn't see or hear anyone else. I just stood in that moment and felt the overwhelming feeling of finishing a huge goal; something I had worked so hard on for the past 10 months. I did it! I just ran 6.2 miles, where 10 months ago, I could not run 100 yards without having to stop. Sorry, Channel 4 News guy ... I know you were trying to ask me about my run, but I was unable to formulate words at that moment.

In these moments, I felt and still feel that this is what it is all about. People need hope and inspiration—including me. As I was running yesterday with over 30,000 people, it struck me. I am not only okay, but I am doing exactly what

I am supposed to. To help others in this life. As I am inspiring others, they are inspiring me with their kind words and gestures. It is a never-ending, wonderful, life giving circle. I believe each one of us has a purpose here on earth, no matter how big or small. I hope others can experience a life with a purpose, for it is a great feeling. I will continue my journey in this life with determination, inspiration and love. There is a saying I keep on my fridge at home. Simply it says;

Life is not measured by the number of breaths we take, but by the number of moments that take our breath away ...

1

The Unexpected

The child possessed so many angelic traits, May thought, because she was born on a Sunday. Labor had not been easy, and the obstetrician had opted to put her to sleep for the delivery. Later, of course, she would suspect why he did this.

As May awakened, she was aware of the sounds of moaning and incoherent babble. The next sensation was one of warmth; her hand was enclosed in that of another. Blinking and trying to clear the fog of anesthesia, she looked up into the face of her husband, Robert. It was over, then, she thought. The baby had been delivered.

Confused and full of growing anxiety, May tried to focus her eyes and looked around for the baby. She saw only the large woman in the next bed, snoring heavily, and an incomprehensible bustle in the hallway beyond. She was drawn back like an anchor to the sadness and pain in her husband's eyes.

"What is it? What's happened?"

He produced a sad smile. "We have a beautiful baby girl, May, but she has some problems."

Feeling the cold, tight fist of fear clench around her heart, May said, "What kind of problems?"

She'd suspected something was wrong throughout the

1

pregnancy. She hadn't quite known why, and the doctors had no explanation for her worry. Everything had seemed fine to them. But she had felt the sharp, awkward kick and had been somehow troubled by an inexplicable foreboding. Only a week before the delivery, she'd gone to Dr. Goldsmith and told him of her concerns. He sent her to the hospital for an X-ray to ease her mind. She'd taken it as a good sign that he hadn't called to alert her of a problem. Now, however, she wondered what he had seen in those X-rays. If he'd known something that it was simply too late to advise her of and if that was why he'd allowed her the reprieve of anesthesia during the birth.

Now Robert explained that the baby's fingers were webbed, and May tried to picture this in her mind, trying to understand what it meant. She'd never heard of such a thing and could not shake the confusion. How could such a thing happen? What did it mean? Surely, though, a problem with the fingers was not significantly detrimental to the child, right?

"Will she be okay? Can I see her?"

Robert nodded. "The pediatricians are checking her now. They can do surgery to correct it. There may be other complications, but she's beautiful, May. She'll be all right."

May felt relief slowly ease the grip of fear but knew she would not be free of it until she saw the baby and held her in her arms. In the anxiety of the moment, she had not recognized the uncertainty in her husband's voice or known that he'd said the baby would be all right not only to reassure her but also to convince himself that it might be true. She understood much later that what he did not tell her was for her own good. She would not have been able to comprehend it all in that moment.

The obstetrician came in next, and May turned to him, hopeful that he would be able to offer further reassurance.

Dr. Goldsmith stood beside the bed and smiled kindly. "I take it your husband has explained some of our concerns about your daughter. Before the nurses bring your baby in, I wanted to talk to you about her condition. I have to tell you that we don't know much at this point, and I know it must be terribly frustrating for you. What we do know is that she appears to be otherwise healthy and that there's no one to blame for this. These things happen, and we don't understand why, but I know you did all you could to make sure this was a healthy pregnancy. There are amazing things that can be accomplished through surgery these days. There's much reason to be optimistic."

He reached out and put a hand on May's, giving it a gentle squeeze. May felt the tears in her eyes just before they slipped down her cheeks. She had not realized how much she needed to hear these words: that she was not to blame for whatever was wrong with her daughter. Still, the thought wedged itself in her consciousness and would be the single unanswered question that would revisit her throughout her life.

Why?

When the doctor left, there was little to say. Robert and May clung to each other's hands like a lifeline. The sounds of the busy recovery room pervaded all of May's senses, and she closed her eyes. Still groggy, she slipped into a restless slumber and was only awakened when she was moved to a semiprivate room. With waking came anxiety.

The minutes passed slowly, and finally the door opened. A nurse came in carrying a small bundle in a pink blanket. May recognized the woman as the nurse who had been with her during the delivery. Her name was Marty. She held the baby close and walked to the side of the bed where she lowered the infant into May's waiting arms. All May could see of the child was a head of black hair and a sweet, perfect face. The miracle of the tiny baby in her arms erased all of May's concerns. She felt only love and peace.

When the baby blinked and opened her big, brown eyes, May smiled at her and kissed her head. She looked so normal. How was it possible that anything was wrong with this child?

The nurse stood by, expectantly. Robert remained next to the bed, allowing for the moment of bonding between mother and child. Then May delicately pulled back the corners of the blanket to reveal the tiny hands that looked like mittens. A flood of thoughts filled her mind. She'd never known such a thing was possible. She wondered many things but mostly, *Why? Why? Why?* She continued to unwrap the blanket, touching the baby's soft skin with her fingers and releasing the tiny, kicking legs. And then her heart thudded, and her chest tightened. Something was horribly wrong. There were no thoughts then because none of what she saw made sense. The baby's right leg was misshapen and very short below the knee. The foot was turned inward and had too many toes. She stared for a moment, trying to comprehend, and then she looked up, a question written on her face.

There were tears in her husband's eyes, which were glued to the baby. The nurse was silent, but tears streamed down her cheeks.

May turned back to her daughter. "Why didn't you tell me?" she asked, speaking to no one in particular. Even as she said it, she knew the answer. It was easier for her this way, with the baby in her arms, to understand that there was no changing what was; there was only acceptance.

The cloud of unreality and disbelief still clung to the moment, however, and the unanswered questions were almost too much to bear. Only in the baby's eyes did May find any relief from the turmoil in her mind. Afterward, when the baby was fed and Marty came to take her back to the nursery, she bent down and hugged the young mother.

"It is difficult," she said. "It always is, but love wins out. You'll see. She'll be the light of your life, and that's something to be thankful for."

As she was leaving the room, Marty turned back and said, "I have such a special feeling for this baby. She's brightened my heart like she'll brighten many more."

They named the child Betsy.

Word traveled fast about the new addition to the Burch family. Not only was the maternity ward buzzing about their newest charge, but the residents of that small town in southern Georgia were gathering themselves up and preparing to lend their support.

The following day, May woke in a private room with her mother beside her. The comfort of her mother's presence was worth more than any words, and the two women sat together in knowing silence. May knew the obstetrician must have pulled some strings to get her there when the rest of the maternity ward was full to max capacity.

As the morning sun began filtering through the blinds, the visitors began to arrive. Throughout the day, a steady stream of friends, family, neighbors, churchgoers, and well-wishers came to see Betsy and to give May and the Burch family their love. It was breathtaking for May, and there were tears—many tears—but there were even more open arms and blessings showered on little Betsy.

In the middle of the afternoon, Robert came into the room with a grin that May had not seen since before the baby was born.

"Can you stand and walk to the window?" he asked.

"What are you up to?"

"I want you to see something."

Tentatively, May stood up and let her husband guide her by the arm to the window. He pulled open the blinds and said nothing. He didn't have to. Outside her first-floor window, May saw people milling about and talking, lining up at the entrance of the maternity ward. All of them were there to see Betsy and shower the new mother and baby with support. Tears sprung to May's eyes and spilled over.

Robert hugged her. "It'll be all right. It'll be all right," he whispered.

For the rest of the day, the operator in the main lobby had to call over to the maternity ward to advise them to keep the visitors moving so that a line didn't form at the entrance.

One of the last to visit was the pastor of First Baptist Church of Albany, a man May knew to be quiet, caring, and understanding. He paid his respects and congratulations and laid one hand on May and one on Betsy, who slept in her mother's arms. "May, there was only one perfect human ever born."

The wave of his words washed over May, and she found peace in them. It was in moments like these that she knew there was peace to be found in the situation, but there was also no end to the heartache.

The flowers filled every available surface, and the room reeked of the sweetness of huge yellow chrysanthemums and pink roses. May's mother had left the hospital and was stationed at the Burch house where additional visitors were dropping off food and gifts for the new baby. She called once to let May know that there was so much food she'd had to start freezing it.

The next morning, May woke up alone. *Somebody help*, she thought. *Will she be able to walk, write, function normally, have a long, full life?*

Later in the morning, when Betsy was curled in her mother's arms again, the pediatrician came into the room and gave voice to the one thing that May dared not think.

"These are, of course, only the visible defects," he said gently but no less earth-shatteringly. "There may be others that we cannot see."

After that, there was nothing but an overwhelming cloud of depression. *How long will it be for the answers to come? How will I care for my other children and deal with this as well?* And even more difficult to put words to: *Will she die? Is there so much wrong with her that she won't live?* May prayed with urgency then, overwhelmed by the impossibility of handling this—any of it—on her own. *Please let her live, God. Don't take her from me. Please.* A fierceness seemed to take hold of her as she prayed, and she was reminded of a similar moment, years ago. She'd already lost one baby, a premature infant who went to heaven not long after birth. *I can't do it again. She's my baby. I want her. I need her. I can't lose her too.*

Later that day, May received a pre-planned tubal ligation and woke up from the anesthesia in the evening. A high full moon was already filtering its pale light into the room. Shadows fell around the sweet-smelling flowers, and everything was so peaceful and quiet that May thought perhaps she hadn't made it through the surgery and this was heaven. Then she felt the tiny movements of the baby on her chest and smiled. This was not heaven, then, because this baby was meant to live.

May's mom and dad were both in the room when she woke, and her mother's quiet strength was contrasted with her father's beaming pride over his new granddaughter. Neither of these, she suddenly thought, could she do without.

Coming out from under the cloud of anesthesia, May became aware of the pain. Her entire midsection was sore and made for a very uncomfortable night. Still, Marty had displayed her usual compassion and left Betsy in the room to sleep with her mother through the night. Even waking and feeding the baby was a balm to May's body and soul.

In the morning, the orthopedic surgeon came, bringing fresh pain to May. May and Robert had been told that he would be visiting but not when. When he came into the room, May was alone and had no idea who he was. Finding out, however, she was immediately optimistic that answers to their numerous questions might be forthcoming. Her hopes were quickly dashed, not only by what he said but by his manner in general. The doctor walked into the room brusquely, without so much as a cordial greeting. He proceeded to describe the examination he'd done on Betsy that morning as impersonally as if he were reading out of a medical text.

"I'm not going to lie to you. The defects are severe. There

will be a long lineup of surgical procedures in her future—a dozen on her hands alone—and even then it's not reasonable to expect that there won't be complications. Every surgery opens up the possibility of infection. And as far as the leg ..." Here he lifted a page on Betsy's chart and shook his head, "I don't think it's worth trying to work with what's there. Amputation is the likeliest option."

Throughout his speech, May sat upright and motionless in the bed, stunned beyond words. A mix of fury and sadness welled up inside of her, knowing that she did not deserve to have this callous man fill her with fear and toxic pessimism. She withheld any show of emotion until he left, and then the entirety of her many days of pain, fear, worry, and doubt overwhelmed her, and she cried with abandon. She was nearly hysterical when Marty came into the room and instantly put her arms around May and began calming her.

The two women sat together for a while.

"I feel your pain," Marty said. "I've had my share too. I had a daughter, a beautiful baby girl like yours. When she was born, the doctors told me something was wrong with her heart, but they had no answers. It was a torment for me, but I trusted in God as much as I could and felt that peace would somehow come to us. She grew, and she filled my life with joy, but she didn't flourish. The answers came, and they were not what I wanted to hear. She was so very sick." Marty paused to wipe a tear away. "She left us when she was three years old. She was a precious gift—a miracle to us—and I am forever grateful that we had her for as long as we did. In the end, peace came to her, and for that I must always be thankful. I see your little girl—I see Betsy—and feel the same love I have for my daughter. I like to believe in the great possibility that her life represents."

With this, hope bloomed again, and May understood that the blessing of the people around us and the goodness of human compassion in the face of adversity is a daily miracle. She also took comfort in the kindness of her obstetrician who talked of releasing her and Betsy the following day. His eyes seemed to reflect her pain, and his gentle manner was a simple but effective acknowledgment that he understood and respected her needs.

When he last visited, her pastor had said, "We believe in miracles, but to experience them we must remain strong and not allow despair to claim us. Be patient with people and understand that they often won't know what to say. This is not a sign of apathy but quite the opposite. You will find, through this, that there is more good in people than you would otherwise have known."

Later, May would appreciate this as one of the wisest things anyone had ever said to her.

2

A Place among the Rest

The day of the Cooper River Bridge Run dawned bright and beautiful on an April morning in Charleston, South Carolina. I woke up with a start, knowing that this was the day I'd waited for, planned for, trained for. Eric made us breakfast and talked about the day ahead. Full of nervous energy, we decided to walk the mile from my house to the starting line. Once we were outside, the fresh air was invigorating and filled me with optimism and excitement.

The bridge itself is two and a half miles long, connecting Charleston to Mount Pleasant, where I lived. It crossed the Cooper River in the Charleston Harbor. I hadn't lived in Mount Pleasant long before I discovered the Bridge Run and met Eric. Now we walked together under the dappled shade of the oak trees, and I found peace in the beauty of the trees, with the Spanish moss gracefully hanging down from the tangled limbs.

I turned the corner to see the ballasts of the Ravenel Bridge rising into the sky. Ahead of us was Coleman Boulevard, and we could see the road markers closing off the street to traffic and containing the multitudes of people that were already gathering for the race. That's when the nervousness really set in, along with the doubts. I walked forward on my everyday prosthetic while

Eric carried the running blade. The plan was for me to change into the running blade prior to the start of the 10K. It was not easy to walk on the running blade. It was specifically made for running and didn't provide much support as far as a heel is concerned. To wear it was like walking on tippy-toes—uncomfortable for general mobility but optimal for running.

The news reporters later confirmed a crowd of nearly 40,000 for race day, but as we stood there on that early spring morning, all we discerned was the palpable energy radiating off of the gathered runners. Music started playing from tents located nearby, and we located the area where we were to start.

We had checked in a couple of days prior and received our starting packet, including our assignment to group G, which informed us where to begin the actual 10K. We had received our running numbers in the packet, which I now wore proudly on my shirt. It was a reminder of the hard work and dedication I committed to over the past months in preparation for this day. I pondered if this number meant the same to everyone, specifically the professional runners around me. It was probably just another number to them, another 10K race. But to me, it was a trophy of accomplishment.

We arrived at the starting section for group G early and found a shady tree to wait under. I sat and removed my everyday prosthetic that was attached just below the knee to my right leg. Eric knew the drill and held out the running blade with the words "No Excuses" emblazoned in pink around the laminated frame. While I placed this deftly in the empty space, I watched as he maneuvered my everyday walking leg into his backpack. Catching my eye, he winked and cinched up the pack so only the foot stuck out, adorned with my other running shoe.

I laughed at this, and he proudly tossed the pack onto his back as I finished attaching the prosthetic that I would run with. He helped me to stand. I bounced a little on the running blade and noticed that already the leg in the backpack was getting some interested looks. Most of the passersby looked at it, confused, and then looked at me, down at my leg, and finally the smile of recognition dawned. Eric enjoyed this immensely and joked to one or two interested parties that I had a "leg up" on the competition.

Music was being played to pump up the runners, and it filtered through the crowd. The excitement in the air was contagious, and everyone was happy and talkative. Time passed quickly, and an announcement was made for the runners in group G to prepare and gather at the starting line. I smiled nervously at Eric, who looked as calm as could be. Each running group was huge, and we moved en masse to the starting line on Coleman Boulevard. We organized so that each runner had some space. I took a deep breath.

Me and Eric prior to start of 10K

Pressing down the number pinned to my shirt, I thought of how odd the human condition is; how we are at once anonymous and yet wholly individual, fueled with an unlimited capacity for understanding and overcoming our own struggles. Time slowed to nothing but the rush of my breath, the beat of my heart, and a voice beside me as Eric said, "You've got this," and I couldn't help wondering if I did, even though I knew I had no choice but to try.

3

A New World

I remember the hospitals and the bandages. I have bits and pieces of these memories: the huge, plaster casts on my arms and the frustration of not being able to move freely. Cold X-ray tables. The radiology department was always cold, and the metal table scared me. I was terrified of the doctors taking out my stitches. Mostly, I remember waking and seeing my mother beside me. I remember coming home.

I had a blue bedroom, and my grandmother would come check on me there. Before the amputation, I still had my lit-

Me and Aunt Adele, Dauphin Island.

tle foot, and I could only walk unevenly. My mom's sister, Aunt Adele, arranged a trip to Dauphin Island, and I walked on the beach and felt the love of the people around me. The next thing I remember was being in the hospital. But it was all just something I had to get through. After that, there were the visits to the prosthetics office on the main street that bisected downtown Atlanta. Through it all, my mother was nothing but supportive. I never saw her cry.

The first weeks of my life were a turmoil of emotions for everyone who loved me. My mom reflected back on those days with me often as I got older. Once we were home from the hospital, she told me, life returned to some sort of normalcy. But not the one my family was used to. It was a new normal. Mom returned to this life as a new mother of three and was immediately swept up in the routine.

Before long it was February, Valentine's Day. John and Sara Lynn both had parties at school, and Mom committed to helping out, not wanting my siblings to feel that all of the attention was going to me, their new baby sister. On top of that responsibility, she came down with a fever the night before the party and had to make a quick stop by the obstetrician in the morning to find out why her breasts ached so painfully.

Dr. Goldsmith, with his habitually calm and attentive bedside manner, assured her that she was suffering from a breast impaction, common in new mothers, and recommended that she stop nursing me. It was disappointing to her, but she knew it had to be done.

Adding this to her tasks for the day, Mom went home and tried to give me a bottle for the first time. I would have none of it. Mom was frustrated at first, trying to get the bottle anywhere near my mouth, but I kept turning away.

After a few moments of frustration, she started giggling as she stared down at me gazing up at her with wide, questioning eyes. Instead of forcing it, she leaned back in the recliner with a great sigh. It was a rare moment of quiet in an otherwise busy day, and she was determined to take advantage of the down time with me. I lay there calmly in her arms, always the contented baby. I wouldn't take a pacifier, which she found interesting. My brother, John, was so attached to his that she used to joke that he might go to college with it. Then, at five years old, he was finally rid of the thing, and there I was, a new baby who spit the pacifier out and soothed myself.

In the coming days, Mom was exhausted and hurting. In addition to being up throughout the night with a newborn who had difficulty feeding from a bottle, she was in pain from the impaction. And for the first time since I'd been born, she allowed herself to feel bitterness. It welled up and overflowed in great quantities of tears throughout the following days, whenever she was alone. And in those emotional hours, she questioned the justness of it all even while she felt she had no right to question God so much. But there were not enough answers. She hated what I would have to face. And the worst part was that she didn't even know the extent of what that would be.

A month after my birth, Mom took me to my first appointment with the pediatrician. On the way, she recanted on her feelings from the previous days, sorry that she'd entertained such doubts about God's plan. She still ached for her child, but her faith was renewed that in time the answers would come, and they would be her hope.

My grandpa—Mom's father—called that morning after the appointment and asked after me, calling me his special granddaughter.

"I wish I could give her my leg, May. You know that," he said to my mom.

"We all would, Dad. I hate to think of her ever suffering."

"You know what I think? I think we suffer when we expect that life owes us more than we're being dealt. She won't expect that. Maybe that's the fortunate thing about her condition. She'll never know otherwise, and so she'll see only the blessings and be thankful for those."

He always had a gentle touch with words, and it was in moments like those that my mom was grateful for the love and support of her parents, who always seemed to offer just the right encouragement.

My pediatric appointment had relieved some of her concerns as well.

"On the surface," the doctor had said, "everything seems normal."

Mom took this to heart. She knew deep down that nothing else was wrong with me. Aside from the obvious physical defects, I was a normal, healthy baby. Mom would deliberately confirm this to herself often in the days to come. The doctor also gave her great reports of Scottish Rite Hospital in Atlanta where I would likely have the first of many surgical procedures. Mom left the office with me feeling that God was in control and would guide us in the right direction. We would all just have to take it one day at a time, and everything would be all right. But then, doing that had never been one of her virtues.

Another month passed, and Mom was dreading our visit with the orthopedic surgeon, Dr. Coleman. Ever since his devastating, postpartum speech to her, she'd been leery of going near him in a potentially fragile state. When he finally stepped into the exam room, she had hardened herself to his callousness. It was, nonetheless, a challenging visit.

"I took her to the pediatrician," Mom began. "He said she's quite healthy."

"Well, she may be, but as I told you, there will be extensive surgeries. I feel your best option is to go to Scottish Rite Hospital in Atlanta for these. I took her X-rays to an orthopedic convention last week, and the general consensus is that the doctors there will be best able to handle the severity of the problem ..."

Again, the mention of Scottish Rite Hospital. Mom felt strongly that we were being led to the doctors there. She was at least glad that this meant Dr. Coleman would have no reason to ever lay a hand on me in an operating room. While this thought satisfied her, it did not give her the last word. Dr. Coleman stood up to leave, condescension written on his face as he looked at the little baby in Mom's arms.

"It's a good thing there are doctors over there who will do this," he said. "I wouldn't touch it with a ten-foot pole."

Unable to think of the words quick enough that would put him in his place, Mom just rolled her eyes and stewed for a minute.

At home, the support was much more forthcoming than it was in Dr. Coleman's company. Letters, phone calls, and visits were still in abundance as people learned of my condition and continued to pay their respects to our family. Particularly heartening was a letter Mom received that afternoon from her Sunday school teacher, Nena.

> Dear May,
> Thank you so much for calling me on Saturday and giving a report on Betsy. You know we are all so very interested in hearing of her progress. We missed you at the Sunday school class meeting last night, but we each prayed for the Burches in our own way. God knows, hears, and answers ...

Moments like those reminded my mom that there were so many small blessings to be thankful for.

One morning in the middle of March, we set out for the Scottish Rite Hospital for Crippled Children in Atlanta. Mom and Dad were in the front seats, and I was in my car seat in the back. From our hometown of Albany, the hospital was three hours away, and making the drive with a three-month old baby was hardly ideal for my parents. Fortunately, my grandparents had been able to come to town to stay with my siblings, John and Sara Lynn, so there was some peace for Mom and Dad in knowing that they could focus on me while the other children were well cared for.

As we got closer to our destination, Mom's nervousness began to mount. I started to get fussy as if I too could sense the uncertainty of what we faced, or perhaps just the tension in the car. Mom held me in her arms to comfort me in those days before seat belt laws, and her heart pounded as we pulled up to the hospital. She found herself wondering if she was really ready to get the answers she'd been longing for or if it would be better to go on not knowing exactly what lay ahead for me.

The hospital itself was a traditional Masonic building, Palladian in style with two long white wings on either side for the boys' and girls' wards, respectively. Upon entering the building, my parents were surprised at how much bigger it appeared from the inside. We were greeted by a nurse, and I was checked in while my parents waited nervously and tried to peer into the wards.

It wasn't long before they took us back, beyond the nurses' station and into the girls' ward where a smiling young nurse directed us to the bed that was to be mine. It was a crib-style bed, large and made of metal, with bars that could be raised and lowered. Efficient certainly, but it reminded Mom of a cage.

My parents settled me in the bed and sat beside it, hardly daring to speak. What they saw around them was like a glimpse into an unknown world. All along the large corridor were beds and children afflicted with a myriad of deformities. There before them were children with problems they could never have imagined. Beside many of these kids were bewildered-looking parents who, like themselves, wanted only answers and a dose of hope. Other children were alone, attended only by nurses and other staff who moved around them efficiently but with much care. I was clearly the youngest of the children but by no means the most severe of the cases, which both heartened and disturbed my parents.

To my mom, it was evident that both she and my dad were overwhelmed, but they turned their attention to the child between them. I was waking as the doctor approached us. He was the first in a string of pediatricians, lab staff, X-ray teams, and dieticians who made their observations and visited with us throughout the morning. By midafternoon, my parents were exhausted and grateful that I was asleep after the ordeal of so many strangers poking and prodding at my body.

One of the nurses approached and whispered kindly, "I can stay with her. Why don't you two go get some lunch? There's a cafeteria at the back of the main building there."

Mom was pleased with the kindness and the offer, and she and my dad allowed themselves that brief reprieve. Once they were gone, however, they found it difficult to be away. Hurrying through their lunch, they returned to the ward in only twenty minutes. What they saw there brought tears to my mother's eyes.

The nurse was standing beside the bed while I slept. A resident stood over me with a camera, taking pictures of every part of my body. Mom looked away and blinked back the tears, fighting the sudden urge to pick me up and run as far away as she could.

Afterward, the nurse smiled apologetically.

"We'll be needing X-rays too. It might be best if we try to do it while she's sleeping."

Of course I didn't stay asleep for long. As soon as the technicians placed me, in only my diaper, on the huge metal X-ray table, I woke up and began wailing at the top of my lungs. Mom made a move to retrieve me, but an orderly put his hand on her arm.

"It will be best if we just try to get this done quickly. Then you can hold her."

Seeing me lying helpless on the table, dwarfed by the huge machines overhead, was too much for my dad. He stepped out of the room. In another moment, it was all over, and the day wore on.

Twelve hours later, a kindly gentleman in a pristine white coat approached and introduced himself to my parents as Dr. Lovell. He was the head pediatric orthopedic doctor at Scottish Rite and very well respected in his field. He shook hands with Mom and Dad and sat beside them at my bedside. He had a soothing manner as he delivered the first comprehensive descriptions of my condition that my parents had heard in the three months since my birth.

"The condition here is called *syndactylism*," he said, pointing to my hands, "meaning that the fingers are webbed together. The little leg has no tibia, which is the long bone in the lower leg, but the fibula—the short bone—is there, and an ankle joint is also present, which may bode well for future surgeries. You can see that the foot on this affected side has extra toes, and some of these are also webbed. The good news is that the other leg has both bones and seems perfectly normal."

He paused here and smiled at my parents, understanding probably that it can be difficult for parents in these situations to come to terms with such a comprehensive list of defects. In another moment, he continued.

"I know that your main concern must be what all of this means for Betsy and for you. I can tell you that we have some wonderful doctors coming to see her. We'd like to keep her here overnight for observation and then have you visit with Dr. King and Dr. Bayne tomorrow. Dr. Richard King is an orthopedic surgeon, and Dr. Louie Bayne is a hand surgeon. Both are renowned experts in their respective fields, and they can tell you everything you want to know about corrective procedures and what the future will hold for Betsy."

Mom appreciated the professional and stately man who sat before them. His gentle manner exuded an understanding of her feelings and gave her much reassurance that the difficulties God had given me were not unheard of. Moreover, Dr. Lovell made her feel that we were in exactly the right place to face the many challenges that lay ahead.

As soon as he was gone, though, my parents were left alone to face all that they had been told. Somehow, it was never enough. There were still so many uncertainties. Looking around, my mom saw that at the end of each bed was a card with a diagnosis written on it and slipped into a clear sheath.

She glanced at the placard at the end of my crib: "Multiple Congenital Anomalies," it read. *I am a mother of a child with multiple congenital anomalies*, she thought. *A child with syndactylism, a missing bone in the leg, and … what else?*

The following morning, my mom returned to the hospital early and found the nurses caring for me. I was quickly placed in her arms, and the head nurse informed her that Dr. Lovell would like to see us first thing. When he arrived, they brought me into one of the small rooms at the end of the long ward, behind the nurses' station. Four residents soon filtered through the door and introduced themselves. They began to evaluate and assess my problems, and Mom had no idea what was going on. Dr. Lovell saw the confusion on her face and crossed the room to stand beside her. Leaning over, he whispered, "This is a learning experience for them. They will be the doctors that will work on cases like hers in the future."

It helped Mom to know that Dr. Lovell sensed her uneasiness, and his nearness gave her strength. When the residents were done examining me and touching my hands, legs, and feet, they stepped outside to discuss their findings and conclusions with Dr. Lovell. Mom could hardly wait, as usual, to hold her little girl. I curled up in her arms again and took my bottle greedily. Mom smiled, thinking that even in this I had made such progress.

"You'll be just fine. You'll see," she cooed and gazed into the big brown eyes of her sweet baby.

A moment later, Dr. Lovell returned to the room and told my

mom that he had scheduled visits with Dr. King and Dr. Bayne. We were to visit Dr. King at his office in downtown Atlanta that morning, and Dr. Bayne would observe me there, at the Scottish Rite Hospital, later that afternoon. Eager now for progress, Mom headed out to pick up my dad at the hotel so they could take me to meet with my new orthopedic surgeon.

4

A Pace of Her Own

The excitement of the announcer for group G got my adrenaline pumping even more. It was surreal once we got going. The run started on Coleman Boulevard, two miles from the base of the bridge. My nervousness turned into energy, and I was on my way.

The first few steps past the starting line were ones of pride and exhilaration. My exhilaration would soon turn into determination as the race wore on, and that same determination inside of me that I knew so well would help me finish the race. As I moved into a steadier pace, I noticed there were people all around me, yet I felt as if I had the whole road to myself.

Eric kept pace beside me and snapped a few pictures off. I tried not to laugh and throw off my breathing. I tried instead to remember everything he'd told me as we'd practiced on the track. Ahead, I could see the towers of the Ravenel Bridge growing taller as I moved closer to its base. I knew the incline was approaching.

The week before, we had done a trial run across the bridge and then back again, as part of our training. We'd begun our preparation barely nine months before, at the end of August, not long after we met. I had told him of my interest in running a 10K.

It was something I needed to do, I'd said, a desire that came to me like a lightning bolt.

When I met Eric, I was new to the area but had heard about the annual Cooper River Bridge Run. Knowing my desire to run and the fact that I hadn't been able to accomplish it up to that point, he was as motivated as I was to check this challenge off my list.

"It's in April?" I had asked him. "Do you think I can be ready by then?"

Although he was a firefighter and in great shape, Eric had told me he hadn't run a marathon since high school and that it would be an accomplishment for him too.

"I think you can. I think *we* can." He smiled, and it was the start of something. Something wonderful and exciting, and something that would bond us and blossom into a beautiful relationship.

The first half mile was a time of introspection, and I began going back in time in my mind, thinking of my childhood and the tough times I went through. This reminiscence left me feeling nothing but grateful; I knew it was those struggles in my life that placed me in this exact moment. I reflected on conversations my mom and I'd had through the years, truly appreciating her struggles as well. The ballasts of the bridge were still distant, but with each step, they grew closer. I felt brave, bold, dauntless, even though there were challenges enough ahead of me.

5
Angels on Earth

Throughout my first year, the days of harsh medical realities were tempered with bouts of normal life at home. Yet there was at all times a vague undercurrent of anticipation.

Spring arrived, and my family spent Easter in Ocala, Florida, with my mom's parents. When she stepped off the plane holding me, Gran and Grandpa were there exclaiming over how big I had gotten and how alert I was now, at four months old. The week was spent in ease and comfort.

Mom recounted our visits with the specialists to her parents as the family gathered around the table for dinner on the first night. Somehow she felt it was easier to grasp the reality of the situation within the warm embrace of family.

"Well, we didn't exactly get the definitive answers we were looking for, but Dr. King offered several possibilities for how to proceed with the leg. There will be prosthetics we can get for her when she begins to walk that will fit onto the existing leg, but other than that, we just have to wait until the hand surgeries are completed. He wanted to look over the X-rays and see her again in three to four months. He said there are new innovations all the time, so waiting might work in our favor, although the impatient part of me wants it all done now.

"Dr. Bayne was wonderful. He said he's only seen five cases similar to Betsy's in the past fourteen years, but he thinks hers will not be as complicated as some since all of the fingers are side by side. Some children are born with the fingers in a fist, and it's very difficult then to save them and give the fingers the length they need. He wants to begin in about five months, and he'll operate on both hands at the same time, separating the thumbs first."

She teared up while she was talking, but my dad reached over and put a hand on hers.

"You know, this will be the best thing for her. Just think how nice it will be to see her using those fingers," Grandpa said.

They looked at me where I lay in the bassinet, cooing and waving my little, mitten-like hands.

"Do you feel confident in the doctors?" Gran asked.

"Yes. Especially Dr. Bayne. He has a wonderful, easygoing manner, and I liked him a lot."

Throughout the rest of the visit, it was clarified for my mom that she had many reasons to be thankful for the family and friends who looked at me and saw only my beauty and none of the defects.

When we returned home, Mom was asked to speak to her women's group on faith.

"Who better than you?" Nena had asked her.

Mom knew that she had insight to offer. Her faith had seen her through so much already.

She came home and began planning her words. She knew firsthand how God always seemed to fill her with that inner strength she needed in times of difficulty. She would talk about me, of course.

Flipping through the Bible that night, she landed on a scripture that called out to her: "Why are ye so fearful? Have ye no faith?" (Mark 4:40).

One night later that week, the phone rang. When Mom picked it up, she was surprised to hear Marty's voice on the other end. The nurse who attended Mom after my birth had visited us several times in the first months that we were home, but with all that had happened since, she and Mom talked less frequently.

"I was just looking at my calendar, and it's the month of May, so I thought of my dear friend May of course. I'd love to visit with you and Betsy," Marty said.

They agreed to meet the following day at our house, and when Marty arrived, my mom greeted her with a hug. When she saw me, Marty couldn't help exclaiming over how much I had grown and changed since she last saw me. They sat and talked for a long while.

It was in this conversation that Marty told my mother the truth about Dr. Coleman, who had so offended my mother both at the hospital after my birth and at my later follow-up appointment.

"I didn't want to tell you at the time," Marty said, "because I know how his visit affected you. But I know why he was so bitter and cruel. He came into the nursery earlier that morning to check Betsy, and while he was there, he said, 'I don't understand why God would let a baby like this live when mine was perfectly healthy and died.'"

Mom was shocked and hurt to hear this, but Marty went on.

"I asked around to some of the nurses, and I learned that he lost his own child to SIDS. It made him very bitter. After his visit to your room that day, your obstetrician, Dr. Goldsmith, confronted Dr. Coleman and gave him hell for it. He lit into him with both barrels, telling him he had no right to talk to you at all, let alone make the comments he made."

This gave my mom some comfort, and she was glad Marty had told her. She understood better now, but it did nothing to make Dr. Coleman's behavior excusable. Thinking about strength and faith lately had made her understand that we must draw strength from adversity. We cannot let bitterness win. It will devour us.

Marty's comments about Dr. Goldsmith's response only confirmed what Mom already knew about the man. She could see that there are people who perpetuate good in the world and people who perpetuate bad. I would encounter both as I grew up, but at that time in my life, my mother could only hope that the good would have more influence.

The surgeries began that summer of 1973, when I was six months old. My parents returned with me to the old Scottish Rite Hospital where I stayed for two weeks. The first surgery was to separate the thumbs, just as Dr. Bayne had recommended. He successfully completed the operation and several more just like it in the coming months.

In January, I turned one, and there are pictures of me sitting in front of a beautiful pink and blue cake with a wide smile, a short, misshapen leg and foot, and small, semidetached fingers. By that time, I was already pulling myself up and trying to stand on the short leg. There was talk of me getting a temporary prosthesis so that I could learn to walk normally.

When I was much younger than I am now yet old enough to understand, my mother would tell me a story that occurred around this time. I was recovering from my second surgery, and she had spent the day with me at the hospital. It was difficult for my parents to do that at the time since the hospital was three hours away and every surgery meant a hospital stay of several weeks. Fortunately, they had some good friends, the Johnsons, who lived nearby, and my mom would stay with them. That year, she spent Thanksgiving with them and drove home on the weekends to be with my dad and my siblings.

That particular night, she was driving back to the Johnsons' house from the hospital and became lost. The hospital was in a bad area of Atlanta, and she had parked in an area behind the building that was enclosed in a six-foot-tall, chain-link fence. The security guard would lock it after dark for the safety of the cars inside.

That night, Mom got out late and made it to her car just before the guard locked the gate. The Johnsons' house was about thirty-five miles away, and she knew how to get there and back but without any room for error. Somehow she made a wrong turn and couldn't find her way back to the freeway. It felt like she was going around in circles with no idea where she was. She pulled into a gas station to ask for directions, but back then there was a gas shortage, and filling stations often closed early.

She pulled up to a red light, beginning to panic. At that point, she didn't even know how to get back to the hospital. Suddenly, she was overwhelmed. She leaned her head on the steering wheel and cried. Then, something told her to look up. She glanced to her right and saw a man in the car next to her motioning for her to roll down the window. She put the passenger window down a bit.

"Where are you trying to get to, ma'am?"

"Symrna."

He nodded.

"Follow me. I'll get you on the 285, and I'll turn my blinker on right before the exit you'll need to take."

The light turned green then, and my mother followed him. He did exactly as he said and drove off, somehow knowing that she would know her way from there. And she did.

"Always remember this, Betsy," my mom would say. "God guides us when we're lost."

This story, she'd tell me, was further proof that God's angels are here on earth.

6
The First Step Is the Hardest

The one-year mark was a big one for my parents. The pediatricians who assessed my development said with confidence that I was developing normally for a child my age. It was the only confirmation my mom needed to tell everyone that she had known all along that I was a perfectly healthy child.

Around that time, my parents also decided that the frequent trips to Atlanta necessitated a move. It was too hard on everyone to continue to commute to the hospital there. When I was in the hospital, my mom had to live two lives, torn between caring for me and the rest of the family at home.

Between my third and fourth hand surgeries, my dad got a job working for the Federal Energy Administration—a position he thought would get him transferred to Atlanta. Instead, he was told that he'd be relocating to Savannah. This was a small move in the right direction but mostly meant that our family would have to say good-bye to the wonderful friends who'd loved and supported us in Albany.

Life, however, was always changing, always moving forward. And there were, of course, the many angels who walked through it, crossing our paths once in a while, regardless of location.

Then, in the summer of 1974, my mom was plunged into sorrow once more.

I was doing well, with five independent fingers on each hand after the multiple procedures to separate them. After my last hand surgery in July, Mom went to change my bandages for the first time and saw all of the individual fingers. She couldn't believe she was looking at the same hands that I had first waved around over eighteen months ago.

Dr. Bayne had told her that some of his patients didn't have the option of surgery. He said I was one of the lucky ones. Indeed, my mom was starting to think this was true. Through our frequent visits to the hospital, she had made friends with several parents and children. She'd never known so many sick children existed in the world. And she'd never expected to consider me among the lucky, but she did then, starting with those individually formed fingers.

In August, the rest of my family took a family trip to Naples, Florida. My parents stopped in Ocala to leave me with my grandparents while the rest of the family flew on to Naples to meet with some friends.

When they dropped me off, my grandpa was overjoyed to see me taking some of my first steps. Earlier that year, I had been fitted for an unconventional prosthesis that accommodated my little foot, and I had only recently taken to walking in it. I limped some, and it was clear that we would be making frequent trips to the prosthetist's office for adjustments as I continued to grow. Still, it gave me the ability to be upright and mobile.

"Would you look at that," Grandpa said, and tears showed in his eyes as I took my first steps for him. For him and Gran, who hadn't been able to go through the process in person, this was the culmination of all of the concern and fear and worry that they had shared with my mom during the first year and a half of my life. It was the fruition of their hopes and their prayers.

My parents, along with John and Sara Lynn, left the next

morning for Naples knowing that I would enjoy the time with my grandparents and likely be spoiled in the process. As the youngest of ten grandchildren, I was the apple of their eyes, especially Grandpa's.

On their second day in Naples, Mom received the phone call. Gran had tears in her voice as she told my mom that Grandpa had suffered a fatal heart attack that morning.

Mom sat down on the bed in the hotel room, and it took her several moments to understand what this meant. She could hardly fathom it. Even when she was off the phone and sharing the news with my father and preparing to leave and drive back immediately to Ocala, she could not come to terms with the fact that her dad was gone.

What broke her heart even more was that I would not grow up knowing him or even remembering him and how much he had loved me. He had been my biggest fan and had shared so much faith with my mom as she struggled to keep her spirits up. He hadn't stopped talking about how beautiful I was and telling everyone that he couldn't wait for the day when he would see me running, laughing, and playing with the other children. Gran once told my mom that every time I had another surgery, Grandpa would just sit in his recliner by the phone and wait to hear any news from my mom.

Mom consoled herself only in small, grasping amounts with the fact that he'd at least gotten to see me walk and knew that he was loved, not least of all by me. And in the days that followed, when we were back at home and she was struggling for some sense of peace in her grief, Mom watched me playing outside and climbing up the rungs on the monkey bars and throwing kisses at her, and she knew her dad was there with us. His faith and love would be with her always, and she knew she must remind herself to share it with me as much as she could throughout my life.

In the fall of that year, I went in for another surgery. By that time, I was developing my own personality and put on a show for everyone. I was talking, laughing, and cutting up with the nurses. My attitude did not reflect my mom's anxious mood, but she was thankful for my high spirits. Hospital visits were becoming far more normal for me than for her.

Not so many months before, I would cry and yell for my mom whenever she left my sight at the hospital. I had been terribly frightened of all the nurses, aides, and doctors—except Dr. Bayne whom I seemed to have unmitigated trust in. But now I was learning that fear wasn't necessary. It was a small but significant blessing for us both.

I came back from the procedure that afternoon with bandages on both my right hand and left foot. They had widened the web space between my thumb and index finger and removed the extra toes from my little foot. Afterward, I lay propped up on my pillows, waving to everyone with my good hand and generally improving the mood of everyone around us.

Six months later, my father finally got transferred to Atlanta. After spending only one year in Savannah, his government job gave him the transfer my parents wanted. Still, my mom found herself struggling not to feel lonely amidst so much change. It had been difficult to leave Albany where our family had so many friends and supporters, and now to leave Savannah just when it was beginning to feel like home. But it was the best thing to do. My mom had been raised to face challenges without complaint, and that was what she meant to do, to honor the memory of her father if for no other reason.

Meanwhile, I marched through the hospital, winning over doctors and nurses up and down the corridors on our frequent visits.

I had to get a new prosthesis just before our move, and Mom was pleased that I sat in my seat, as good as gold, while they molded me a new one, which was not a short or easy process by any means. I seemed to realize that there were times like this when uncomfortable things had to happen to make life better in the long run. She admired this perseverance that I'd established at such a young age.

That spring, my mom and I went to a meeting Dr. Bayne was hosting with twenty-five of the top orthopedic specialists throughout the United States. He featured me in his lecture and showed me off. Mom was proud of me, sitting in front of all those doctors, on stage and subject to their clinical scrutiny. At one point, I began to get frightened, so Dr. Bayne held me on his lap and continued answering questions from the audience. This calmed me immediately. The two of us had a special bond.

Afterward, Dr. Bayne received quite a few pats on the back for his work, but he still took the time to speak with Mom about me.

"She's a regular poster child," he said fondly.

The only disappointment of the day was that Dr. Fred Brown couldn't be there. He was a renowned doctor who had recently performed a rare and unproven procedure that the orthopedic surgeon, Dr. King, was thinking of using for me. Dr. Bayne and my mom had hoped that he might be able to meet me and advise Dr. King on the procedures that would be performed on my leg.

In July 1975, we moved to Stone Mountain, Georgia, which was just outside of Atlanta, and almost immediately had a network of neighbors and friends who were aware of my condition and pulling for me. Just after moving into our new home, I went in for another surgery on my right hand and was able to go home the following day. Even so, it made such a difference to my mom to know that John and Sara Lynn were at home close by, and to be able to leave to get some rest without feeling so far from me. Some neighbors brought us a meal when we got home, and friends from church sat with Mom through the procedure. It was a big change from the isolation she'd once felt during those anxious times in the past.

Two months later, I had a similar surgery on my left hand. Mom brought me in the day before my surgery for admittance, where we waited over two and a half hours. We waited and waited while I grew fussy and Mom grew irritable. Finally, after waiting and with no communication from the staff, she picked me up and left.

Upon returning home, a woman from the hospital called to ask why we left. Mom explained to her how poorly organized the staff was and that there was no reason we should have been made to wait for over two hours simply to be admitted. The woman told her that if we came back, they would get us right in. Mom knew she had to do it out of necessity but wished she could have said we weren't coming back. As we returned to the hospital, the hospital administrator greeted us in person and assured my mom that such an oversight would never happen again.

It was difficult enough having to prepare a child for another round of surgery without the added frustration of being ignored and waiting for hours. She hoped they learned something from the incident. She knew she had. She learned that her nerves could be fragile at times like those. She dreaded taking me in to the hospital in the first place, staying awake at nights before each surgery, filled with worry and heartache. Part of her hoped it would all just go away if she left. Her reaction rose from a vulnerable place.

She looked around during our hospital visits and saw all of these families from different demographics and backgrounds, many of whom had no medical insurance and were reliant on the hospital and likely afraid to speak up. And the staff did a wonderful job for these children. The doctors were known for the best orthopedic work anywhere. Some of the children were left for days without anyone coming to see them, but the aides loved them all the same and tried to make them better no matter who they were or where they came from. And each of the people who went there was hurting in their own way, managing untold struggles, each deserving to be treated with dignity and respect.

It wasn't like my mom to speak out about such things, but

perhaps she was changing, she thought. She had just been told that I would have to wear casts on both arms for a month. This taught her that there were things we must accept and things we must advocate for. It felt good to be proactive in the face of something she had no control over. While she was at it, she'd also noticed that the meals they brought to the children were often inappropriate. Most families brought in their own meals for their children instead of feeding them the greasy hospital french fries. Maybe she would have to store that observation and mention it another time.

On January 21, 1976, I turned three years old. My favorite gift that year was a nursing kit, which made a lot of sense given how familiar I was with the nurse routine. I definitely knew what everything was used for, and apparently I subjected everyone in our family to the thorough medical attention that I was so used to getting. For them, it was difficult to be upset by this. My dexterity with the devices in the kit just offered further proof that my hands and fingers were working well. Mom would often stop and watch me play, thankful for miracles.

By that summer, we had been in Stone Mountain for a year. I had learned to ride my tricycle and loved being outside. My parents marveled that the prosthesis didn't seem to get in my way as I tried to keep up with the other kids. I had never known anything different, and perhaps it was a blessing, as my grandfather had said, because it hadn't ever given me a reason to think I couldn't do something.

The prosthesis I was wearing was a new one that I was able to take off and put on all by myself. First, I put on a special, loosely woven sock, then an inner liner made of rubber, and pulled the leg on over it. It strapped above the knee and around the waist. The prosthesis sometimes pinched and rubbed raw spots into my skin in the pressure points and necessitated frequent trips downtown for adjustment. It struck my mom as cumbersome but also a Godsend that allowed me to walk at a normal age. My small foot on that leg stuck out toward the other leg and made for a bit of an awkward appendage. It caused me some pain because I would occasionally hurt the toes on my small foot while riding my tricycle and playing.

In the previous winter, my mom had learned that a new Scottish Rite Hospital would be built, and it was finally completed that summer of my third year. It was in a nice part of town and was an ordinary children's hospital now, serving all types of cases—not just orthopedic. They had me out right after they opened for some publicity and took pictures of me wearing a hard hat and painting a wall. Our family attended the open house, and then, on July 17, my dad and I went on TV to talk about it. They connected me to the hospital and talked about how many surgeries I'd had there. By all accounts, I seemed to enjoy my time in the spotlight.

The best news of the summer, though, came when Dr. Bayne told us he wouldn't need to see me again for a whole year. Mom hardly knew how to feel or what to think. He had been such a fixture in those early years of my life, but now we would be mostly free to go about life as a normal family.

As the long, hot summer days began to wane, Mom went by the church kindergarten with the idea that I might be able to attend school there a couple days a week. At first they said they were full, and then they called later to say that they could take one more student: me. Immediately after she got the news, my mom had a flurry of emotions. Her uppermost worries were how the other kids would react to my differences and how well I would be able to function in a school setting with my unconventional prosthesis. But she needn't have been concerned.

She took me to school on the first day, and I walked right in, completely oblivious to my mother's worries or the reasons behind them. I didn't have a problem then or any day after. I loved school and told my mom often that I would like to go every day like Sara Lynn and John did.

My mom's confession to me, many years later, was that she peeked in at me once or twice in those first days. My motor skills were impressive, and I seemed to love singing the preschool songs. The kids and teachers treated me just the same as everyone else, and even though she was filled with happiness for me, my mom left for home after those visits with tears in her eyes.

We saw Dr. King at the hospital in November. We were beginning to talk about what would be done with my short leg. While we were there, something happened that touched my mom's heart and humbled her. As my mom stepped out into the hallway while I was down the hall having X-rays taken, she saw a little girl step out of the room next to ours with her mother. She had a short little dress on and two artificial legs all the way up to her hips. It took Mom by surprise, and she stared at them. The little girl smiled and said, "Look!" and lowered her head to gaze down at her legs. "Look at my new shoes!"

Mom was stunned but quickly got her senses about her and told the little girl how beautiful they were. It brought shameful tears to her eyes because all she'd seen were those artificial legs, and all the little girl saw were her new patent-leather shoes.

7

Tread in the Dirt

Eric and I had started training by taking it one day at a time, on a track near my home in Mount Pleasant. The first day, I ran a hundred meters and had to stop. But we came back the next day and the next until we had run every day that week. It was a big deal when I finally made it around the track without stopping at the end of the first week. Each week after that, we added a quarter of a mile to the run.

The prosthetic I wore to train was the same one I wore every day. I had visited my prosthetist, Steven, early on, before we'd even started training, to consult with him about the best way to accomplish this goal I'd set for myself. When he suggested that

My running leg, also called Running Blade, with the words No Excuses embedded on it

running a marathon might be difficult with my current prosthetic, he also recommended that I get a running blade. My heart dropped. I had no chance of buying that expensive fitting and told Steven this concern.

"Well, it's not unheard of for prosthetic companies to donate blades to people like yourself. It's a marketing strategy, of course, but you could benefit from their sponsorship. We can check into it if you'd like."

I was on board.

Before long, we had word back from the prosthetics company that a cutting-edge running leg would be on its way. In the two to three months that it would take to arrive, I had no choice but to continue training on my everyday leg.

I was making progress. By the end of October, we were running one mile a day. It was difficult running on a prosthetic that was designed for lighter use, but I couldn't stop training because I had to get at least six miles under my belt by the time the running blade was due to arrive. So I put my head down and did what I needed to do in the interim, keeping my eyes on the finish line.

8
The Gravity of Walking

We had a birthday supper and party for my fourth birthday. It was a fun gathering of family and friends.

Mom said I had such a cute personality those days and talked a blue streak to anyone who would listen. I loved to draw and color and appeared to be left-handed. Mom knew some parents saw this as an impediment in their children and would try to correct it, but four years ago, she couldn't imagine my hands even being usable! I had big brown eyes and long blond hair.

Photo courtesy March of Dimes

I was smart and capable, and Mom could not fathom me growing up with an awkward, clumsy, and unconventional prosthesis for the rest of my life. It would set so many limits on what

I could and couldn't do, and she felt I didn't deserve that. So the decision to go ahead with an amputation and surgery on the leg was made. This decision would allow me to be able to wear the most advanced prosthesis of the time, as opposed to the clunky, makeshift one I would be resigned to if I did not have the surgery. It was painful for my parents and would probably be painful for me, but Mom knew it was the right thing to do, and she knew that she would have to face it with faith and determination for my sake. The surgery was scheduled for that summer.

My parents worked toward helping me understand what would be happening. Before they took me to the hospital in July, I happily told everyone at school that I would be having my little leg fixed. But in the privacy of my hospital room, I tearfully asked my mom, "How are they going to cut my foot off?"

She understood that putting it in such plain terms was my way of understanding it, but it hurt her to hear these words, and it brought all of her doubts forward again.

Apparently unsatisfied, I asked her again if they were going to cut off my foot.

Mom could hardly bear it but tried to explain as best she could what the procedure was trying to accomplish. She knew I was not able to think beyond the mere fact of the amputation, or able to realize what it would be like for me afterward, for the rest of my life. How could she explain it to me when she'd asked "why" countless times and there were no answers? Still, her heart ached as she searched for the right words.

Finally, she said, "We will cry together, but we will also be strong together, Betsy. There is a special purpose for your life, and one day we will know it and be able to understand it all."

Dr. King met with my parents late that afternoon to tell them I was out of surgery and that everything went well. He had in fact decided to perform the Brown method, and that surgery was the first step in what would become a multiple-procedure process. The Brown method was specifically for children who were born without a tibia but with an ankle. The first step involved the amputation of the foot. The second step, which would be done in two weeks, would be to attach the fibula to the small section of tibia that was present. This would create a one-bone leg, leaving the ankle and knee to function normally. It was a rare procedure, and Dr. King was one of few who would do it.

I was in the hospital for several days post-surgery. Dr. King came in to change my dressings. He was fantastic with me. Mom had never seen such a professional at work as he deftly handled a situation that was uncomfortable for all of us. He made sure I looked at my leg and the spot where my little foot used to be. He talked to me about it and told me how much better this change would be for me.

Mom swallowed hard, and her heart raced as she listened. It didn't even occur to her to look at my leg—her eyes were trained on my face, trying to gauge how well I was receiving and processing all of the information.

I was only four and a half and dealing with it in my own way, a way that my parents could not see or understand. And Mom had to remind herself that I had been given the gift to cope with and understand more than most children my age.

Afterward, it was difficult for my mom to fathom that she actually had doubts about whether Dr. King was the right one to perform the surgery. She had every faith in his abilities after seeing me through my first leg surgery. Every recommendation had been that we go with him, and she was pleased that they had made the right choice.

As he was leaving the room, Dr. King turned to her. "God is always merciful with these special little ones and makes it easier for them to overcome. Everything will work out."

My parents brought me home and directly to the den that they had prepared especially for me. They had lined it with blankets and big, soft pillows. I had lots of new toys and gifts that kept me and Sara Lynn busy all day. Mom's sister and brother came for a visit, and the new faces brought joy and laughter to the household after so much worry. It was wonderful to be home and have the support of family.

My recovery went well. Mom took me to Dr. King's office to have my stitches removed, and he was pleased that my leg was healing nicely. He said I could start taking baths again, but I flatly refused. I got upset whenever my mom had to un-bandage my leg. I was frustrated too, at not being able to walk. The next surgery would make this possible, and suddenly my mom couldn't wait for the procedure to be over so that I would begin to see that it was all for the best.

In mid-August, we were back at Georgia Baptist Hospital for the second part of the operation. It had been three weeks between surgeries instead of two as originally planned. However, my mom felt it was a good three weeks of playing and learning together as a family how to deal with my situation. Each day had seemed to ease some of my mental anguish. I had cried and grieved but became gradually stronger and accepting that each day would make a difference. Then, one morning I asked to go out and ride my tricycle.

Mom was overjoyed that I was showing some interest, but at the same time the idea scared her. But what could she say? She watched me climb onto the tricycle all by myself, and off I went with Mom holding her breath and waiting for a fall.

I casually pedaled with just my left leg, with the right one still bandaged and hanging down, apparently unnoticed by me.

In the previous days, we had taken many "walks" around the block, with me in the stroller, and had gone to the movies just for something to do. Mom had seen me frustrated because I couldn't walk, and this made her feel helpless. But finally, after meeting with no hardships on the tricycle, I started scooting around and pulling myself up, even hopping around on one leg. And so we went into the hospital for that second procedure with renewed confidence, faith, and hope.

We had a one o'clock appointment, and I wasn't supposed to eat or drink anything on the morning of my surgery, so Mom and I stayed up as late as we could the night before and ate and ate as much as we could. We giggled together and didn't mention a word about the surgery. It seemed we were all eager to get it over with.

I hit a low point the following morning, however, and asked my mom if they were going to cut off my other foot this time.

Mom felt a chill in her heart as she told me no and tried to explain again what was to be done.

I was in the hospital for a week after the second surgery. After the procedure, I had a rough night with pain and discomfort but then began to recover well.

Within days, I was up in the wheelchair, and Dr. King had brought in the smallest pair of crutches any of us had ever seen. He helped me up out of bed, positioned the crutches under my arms, and … I just stood there. I would have no part of the crutches and refused to even try to use them, which was unusual for me. I only wanted to have the leg propped up with ice on it, so Mom figured it must have been hurting me. She was correct. The throbbing pain that occurred when I stood up was intensified by gravity as my little leg hung down, and it was more than I could bear. I quickly lay back down and placed ice packs on my leg.

In my firm refusal, Dr. King and Mom did not push me to try the crutches. I was tired and emotional, and there was a part of me that just wanted to be normal. I was tired of being in the hospital, tired of surgeries, and wanted to be at home, playing as usual.

On that particular hospital visit, I distinctly remember the nurse who took care of me. Her name I don't recall, but I could easily call her an angel, as she seemed to be sent from above. She was very delicate and nurturing with me and my mom.

I had an IV in my left arm that was causing me much discomfort and pain, enough so that I was in tears about it.

"What is hurting you, my child?" the nurse asked me, probably expecting me to say it was my leg.

"It's this needle in my arm. It hurts ..." I exclaimed through the tears.

As the nurse lifted my hospital gown up over my left arm, the swelling and redness of my arm confirmed my discomfort. The IV fluid was not going into the vein anymore and was infusing directly into the tissues of my arm. The nurse quickly stopped the infusion. She worked with precision and care.

"I'm going to take this IV out of your arm, and it'll feel much better," she explained.

I trusted her completely as I held my arm out to her, knowing she would make it all better. The layers of tape on my arm were numerous, as if someone had kept trying to tape something back together that wasn't working. As the nurse pulled a chair up to the side of the bed to sit on, I recognized that this was not an easy task for her. Her face remained calm, but I could see the frustration in her eyes.

She began slowly peeling back the layers of thick adhesive tape placed by someone who had not considered the delicate skin of a child underneath. She worked diligently and patiently; as the tape stuck to my skin, she applied saline to soak the areas before removing it. This process took many minutes, starting at the top of my arm and working down.

The tears rolled down my cheek, my skin on fire with each delicate pull. The nurse and I looked at each other, with compassion and admiration, and realized in that moment that we would get through this together. She admired my bravery, and I her love and care for me. It was another necessary process: to get through this pain in order to move on to the next step. I will never forget her.

That night, my mom curled up in the miserable recliner next to my bed. However, she recounted later that it was one of the most comfortable in a long line of horrible sleeping positions and inadequate chairs she'd occupied by my bedside.

Oddly, though, those times with me were among her favorite. I had trouble falling asleep right away when the lights were turned out, so we talked instead. That night, I grew quiet, and Mom thought I was asleep. Then my tiny voice reached through the darkness, and I asked, "Mommy, why did God make my leg grow crooked?"

She had to answer around the tears that formed a barrier in her throat. "Betsy, God made us all different. He made you extra special because he knew you were so strong."

"That's true," I conceded. "And when my leg gets better, I'm going to do cartwheels and backbends and ... the splits! And ..."

We spent the next few minutes naming as many things as we could think of until I fell asleep.

In late September, the stitches were removed, and I was back to riding my tricycle with one leg. A couple of weeks before that, Dr. King's X-rays had showed that things were healing nicely and it was time for me to finally get a new prosthesis. We had made several trips downtown for fittings and adjustments. When the leg finally arrived, it was widely admired by my family.

Mom was amazed at how advanced it was compared to the makeshift leg I'd first worn. It was straight and had at the end of it an artificial foot the same size as my real one. It had a waist strap, but it slipped on with my regular sock, and then the socket fit into the leg. It was tinted to be the same color flesh as my other leg, but it was shinier, made of a hard material. The foot was made of a more flexible rubber but still durable. Mom was impressed, but I was not impressed at all.

I totally rejected it. Totally. I crawled or hopped wherever I wanted to go. Mom didn't push or insist, but inside she just wanted to force me to wear it. Instead, it sat propped up next to my bed day in and day out. Sometimes she would bring it downstairs in the hopes that I'd see it there, surprise everyone, and just put it on. No way. There it sat propped against the couch.

I would often stare at my prosthesis as it was propped up on the bed or couch; this was my way of denying the truth. There was a place inside of me that did not want to accept the prosthesis. *Why?* I thought. This was one of many times in my life where that word, that question, would arise. One little tiny word that had so much anguish and sadness attached to it. I was still grieving, in my own way, the loss of my leg after the amputation.

Ever so slowly, I began wearing the prosthesis. It began when Sara Lynn and John joined in and told me that they would play "Mother May I" with me if I wore the leg. And so I put it on for the short game and immediately took it off again. Over the next few weeks, I gradually came to accept the reality of my life; if I wanted to walk, it would require wearing a prosthetic leg.

I would realize later in life that it was at this moment I made the most impactful choice of my life. I chose to win and not be defeated; I chose to wear the prosthetic leg and walk and live my life.

I started back to school, and it helped with my acceptance. We settled into our old routine, and though I did so begrudgingly some days, the leg became more and more a part of that routine.

In addition to this, Mom noticed that my knee seemed to function so much better than it had before. Most importantly to my parents, I seemed happy, and nothing was ever said about the surgeries or any bad memories I may have had of the whole experience.

Months continued to go by, and it was time to visit Dr. Bayne again for a checkup on my hands. Mom couldn't believe it had already been a year since our last visit. I marched in and took over the whole office. They were all happy to see me, and the secretaries let me type on their machines. Dr. Bayne loved it and encouraged me to make myself at home.

As he examined my hands, Dr. Bayne delivered the news that it was time to shorten the thumbs and shape some of my other fingers. Mom knew these were necessary steps. Still, my teacher at school said I was one of the most dexterous children in the class. I was clearly left-handed by then, and already I could spell all of the names of the people in my family and a few others. I was proving to be a quick and eager learner.

Meanwhile, as if life weren't busy enough, Mom began a master's program in education. During our frequent visits to Scottish Rite Hospital, she had befriended the teacher who worked there. The woman had a small office and would spend her days going around to the school-age students and working with them on their studies. It fascinated my mom at the time because she had no idea that such a program or position existed. This got her thinking, and the desire that was raised then did not leave her. She wanted to someday work as a hospital homebound teacher and meant to secure the degree as her first step in that direction. It would take time, but she knew now that most of the difficult early medical decisions in my life had all been made and carried out. My experiences had taught her that with persistence we can accomplish anything.

Time continued to move on, and in 1978, we celebrated my fifth birthday. My parents and even I, to a small degree, knew there would be more surgeries and more trials to come. But as the time in between surgeries grew longer, Mom had more opportunities to be amazed by the girl I was becoming, and I had more opportunities to enjoy a normal, active childhood. I had made such progress in my first five years of life, and the whole experience left my mom incredulous, grateful, speechless, and most of all optimistic about what the future might hold for me.

9

Rising from the Dust

As I approached the base of the bridge, I knew the most challenging part of the run would be the incline. It reminded me again of certain periods of my life and how I always saw the challenges in front of me, and always found the strength and determination to keep going and face them head on. I knew I had Eric beside me and found comfort in knowing I did not have to face this particular challenge alone.

As I looked at the incline in front of me, I took some deep breaths as a little uncertainty washed over me. It was as if Eric knew what I was feeling.

"Just remember, we ran this incline last week, and you did awesome. You are going to do awesome this time too."

I found strength and reassurance in his words. As I looked around, I saw the other participants, each in their own rhythm of running. We were all together but at the same time each in our own world as well. I wondered what those around me were thinking.

My own mind was on the past. At the age of five, I started to remember specific details of my life—memories of surgeries, days in the hospital, the strong bond between my mom and me. As I continued to run, I realized if it had not been for the success of those leg surgeries, I may not have ever gotten to where I was, in that moment, running a 10K for the first time. It was an inspiring thought that moved me, just as my legs were moving powerfully up the incline of the bridge.

10

To March Forward

At the end of the summer of 1978, I was swept up into a whole new world. We had heard of the March of Dimes, which was an enormously popular organization at that time. They were doing great things to increase awareness and fund research on birth defects. There was a lady at church, named Jo, who was involved with the March of Dimes, and she began having conversations with my mom.

Photo courtesy March of Dimes

Jo was a very friendly and warm person. Her hair was white as snow, and she carried herself in a calm yet confident manner. I felt comfortable with her, and I could feel her admiration for my struggles.

I think if my mom learned anything in the early years of my life it was to always be thankful for small kindnesses and offers of help. Learning about the March of Dimes organization was like shining a light in a dark room for my mom. She'd been taking one step at a time for so many years, often stumbling along the way. To learn that there was a whole network of people who knew something about what she and I were going through helped to alleviate so many of the questions and uncertainties that my disabilities raised in her mind and in the way she felt we were perceived by others. She immediately wanted to know more and get involved.

I went with her to meet with the local chapter of the March of Dimes. I was a happy child, and I was used to dealing with doctors, nurses, and adults from church and school. Perhaps more than other children, I was solicited into conversation, questioned, and spoken to with respect and even admiration so often that I was quite comfortable by that time with meeting new people and conversing with grown-ups. The March of Dimes group was delighted with this, and they immediately mentioned that I should consider applying to become a poster child for the local branch.

Between the representatives from the March of Dimes and Jo, I was encouraged and ultimately selected to be the Metro Atlanta March of Dimes poster child in 1979. It was a regional rather than national title, but my mother was excited and imposed on me the importance of helping the organization and others with conditions similar to my own. It would be a responsibility for both of us but certainly one that she felt I was capable of handling. And I already knew that I could do anything because I had the faith and support of the people I loved. I believed in myself because they believed in me.

At the time I was selected as regional poster child, I was still undergoing surgeries on my hands. It was September, and I had been wearing post-surgery splints on both of my hands for nearly a month. It was time to see Dr. Bayne in his office to have the splints removed.

As he removed the splints, my mom and I noticed a brief look of concern cross his face. Dr. Bayne was always calm and filled with love, so the look took us off guard.

"Your thumbs look good, but I would like them to be a little straighter," he said.

As my mom and I looked at each other, sadness washed over me. Dr. Bayne noticed this immediately, as he was so intuitive about me.

"This only means they will improve with patience. They will look great in no time. Everything is fine."

As I heard these words coming from my doctor, whom I held in such esteem, my sadness and questions melted away. I trusted him completely.

It was almost immediately after my visit with Dr. Bayne that I was back in the March of Dimes office to talk with them about my new role as poster child. Mom and I were both enticed by the upcoming experiences they offered. To think, just a few hours ago, we were looking at my newly operated-on hands in the doctor's office, and now we were being told of all these wonderful opportunities this new role would bring. It was quite a contrast but one I gladly accepted. Even as a child, I knew this role was to be taken seriously, as it may help others in need.

As I sat in the office, I spoke with the assembled grown-ups as if I had known them for years.

"She's quite mature and such an outgoing little girl with tons of spirit," Jo commented. Jo, it turned out, would be our liaison in the Stone Mountain district.

I loved hearing such comments, as it only bolstered my fragile confidence as a little girl who saw herself with so many physical differences.

"She is quite something. I am so proud of her," Mom replied.

As we finished up the meeting, one of the representatives approached Mom.

"May, could you write a letter about Betsy, describing her medical condition and background? We would like to do a write-up about her in the local paper here, and it would be very helpful to have your input."

"Of course. I would be honored," Mom replied without hesitation.

A letter about my daughter, Mom thought to herself as she sat down to write. *What can I say about my beautiful daughter? She is very independent and determined. She has always done things on her own, rarely seeking any help. If she makes her mind up to do something, she works at it until she learns how. She has no trauma from her fourteen operations. We have always been honest in answering her questions as to the "whys" of her problems. We have placed her in normal situations and never thought she could not do anything other children could do. Betsy is learning to have good, positive feelings about herself and working on not feeling different from anyone else. She wants to be a nurse when she grows up and work for Dr. Bayne. She loves to swim, despite the stares that she draws, and I would have to say her biggest challenge right now is trying to run as fast as everyone else. At the rate she is practicing, I think it will be soon ...*

The thoughts ran on, and all of them were included in the letter. She summed me up as well as anyone could, for those who had not met me and felt what my mom called my subtle charm in person. She closed the letter by saying she hoped that many people would be benefited by my spirit as she and the rest of my family had been.

An article was written in the local paper announcing me as the Metro Atlanta regional poster child for the March of Dimes. After the announcement in the paper, we began the first of many adventures.

Our first appearance was at the Wyler's Tennis Tournament at the Georgia Tech Coliseum one night in October. Before the tournament started, we were called onto the court and met some of the players. Photographers stood by as I shook hands with

Martina Navratilova. Afterward, I was announced to the crowd for the first time as the March of Dimes poster child for the Metro Atlanta region.

Mom had been worried that I might be overwhelmed by all of the photographers and reporters, but I was perfectly at ease. I heard her telling Jo about my "characteristic grace and poise," without really understanding what this meant. I just loved wearing the banner that bore my title across my chest more than anything. It was our first taste of the publicity that the coming year would bring.

Throughout the activities and appearances we engaged in that fall and winter season, kindergarten was still of number-one importance in my life. I loved it above all else, and it gave me a reprieve from the spotlight. It was where I had space to just be a kid. As Mom's worries about my new role started waning, she was extremely busy clipping local newspaper articles that covered the events I attended. My popularity was growing in my hometown, and Jo stated it would only increase over the course of the year. My mom listened to Jo intently, and so her scrapbooking skills began.

The fall and winter included many events such as marathons, luncheons, walk-a-thons, the Mother's March, and various other venues. There were busy schedules that included many photo sessions with local celebrities, and we were at the beck and call of the March of Dimes and their events in the local Atlanta area, never knowing these local poster-child experiences were preparing us for events on a national level the following year. It was difficult for Mom to imagine what all of these experiences were like for me.

In truth, it was a bit overwhelming as I struggled to make sense of it all. But in doing so, I extracted a general sense of well-being that was more rewarding perhaps than an attention to detail. I saw that it was an honor to be in my position and recognized that I deserved all the recognition I was getting for being strong and brave when I needed to be.

Mom and I had a special relationship where we generally agreed on which days and events were particularly interesting and those that were not. One in particular stood out for both of us. We had realized that local event photo shoots could at times be monotonous and time-consuming. When the March of Dimes arranged a day at Atlanta City Hall with the mayor, we were more than excited to attend. This seemed like perhaps a step above the endless photo sessions with local business people. It wasn't that they were not important; it was just sometimes hard to see a difference was being made with local contributions. Meeting the mayor of the city seemed a bit more interesting and impressive.

As we sat in a private waiting room with a local representative from the March of Dimes, I started to get impatient.

"Mom, when is this guy going to show up?"

One of many bonding moments between me and mom.
Photo courtesy March of Dimes.

I asked, my five-year-old attention span reaching its max.

"Well, *this guy* is the mayor of the city, Mayor Maynard Jackson, and he is very busy. He has made time to meet with us today, and we need to be respectful of his schedule," she said firmly.

Respectful? I just want to go home and play with my dolls, I was thinking. But knowing the seriousness of my mom's tone, I chose to remain silent and continued sitting beside her.

Finally, the door opened, and a gentleman walked in and began introductions. He seemed friendly enough as he engaged in some childlike conversation with me. He took my hand and led me into his office. As he picked me up and set me in his lap, we talked about school and running. All the while, the photographers were strategically coordinating photos of our conversation. Continuing into the council chambers, we listened in on the proceedings. I was finally impressed that the man who'd been so friendly was actually a very important man and not just another kind adult.

The March of Dimes events continued over the following months, and we never quite knew what to expect of them. There was the Mother's March in December, appearances at various events, and of course many photographs of myself with various local celebrities. It was a very busy schedule, and we somehow managed to fit Christmas in and my sixth birthday in January. Mom was a little emotional on my sixth birthday, as it was always hard for her to believe how far we'd come. She was thankful for all that had happened and how well I'd handled it all.

We were approached in February by a March of Dimes representative named Jim. He asked if we had thought at all about having me run for national poster child for the following year. In fact, Jo Malcolm had started talking with my mom about it a while back. She had told her about the extensive travelling tours and the multiple appearances that I would be required to make, but she also told Mom that she thought I was more than capable of handling the demand. Mom had to agree with her on that point.

Now, hearing Jim also put his endorsement on the idea, Mom felt a little stirring of excitement. It would mean missing school for both of us, but she was qualified to teach me on the road. Perhaps it was something to consider more seriously. She told Jim we were interested but would have to think about it more. Mom felt in her heart it was too big a decision for our family to make on our own; she began to pray about it and trust God to lead us on the right path. She knew all of what had happened so far had been possible because she'd turned my life over to Him a long time ago. She'd never seen anything like the way doors had opened for me.

After much prayer and conversation with family and loved ones, it was agreed that the opportunity for national poster child was a once-in-a-lifetime opportunity for me and I couldn't pass it up.

"Betsy, this is a serious commitment. Days of endless travel, pictures, airplane rides, and many more events I cannot even imagine," Mom said to me.

Even at that age, I realized the seriousness of this opportunity. It would mean a year of being away from my siblings and my dad. I knew I would be home in between assignments, but my mom was careful to be realistic about the challenges this presented, and it had me thinking twice.

"Mom, I think I can do it."

I knew in my heart I wanted to, but at the same time, it would require me growing up fast that year. *Will I be able to do what they expect of me? I wonder how many famous people I will meet. How will I go to school?* These and many more thoughts crept through my head.

"I will call Jim and let him know our decision," Mom said as she smiled at me and touched my hand with loving reassurance.

She called Jim on the phone that day and told him that we had all talked about it quite a bit and decided to go ahead and allow my nomination for March of Dimes national poster child to go forward.

Before we knew it, we were having our interviews with the national poster child committee. Up to that point, Mom had been praying and came to the conclusion that the decision must be left with God. Only He knew how much we could take. She knew it would be hard to travel so much—sometimes for weeks at a time. She didn't know the effect this would have on me or our family, but we decided to submit ourselves to His will, and all signs indicated that this was what I was meant to do. The interviews went great and were followed by a two-hour photography session. We met Nancy, the representative who would be travelling with us if I were to get the national title. As I responded very well to all of the attention, Mom continued to be amazed at how well I adapted in such situations.

Over the next couple of months, we continued to make appearances locally for March of Dimes events. Before we knew it, spring arrived, and along with it came blooming dogwood trees, daffodils, and a handful of other springtime flowers. I loved this time of year as I followed my mom around in the yard while she gardened. I would put on her shoes and flop around in the yard. She always enjoyed having my company in the garden.

"Betsy, we have the Superwalk next week. It is an important event and one of the largest for the March of Dimes in this area."

"I'll be ready," I said.

"You definitely won't be wearing those." She chuckled as she looked down at my shoes, seeing me wearing her shoes, more than twice the size of my feet. She was always amazed I was able to put on shoes like anyone else. I never let my prosthetic foot hamper my desire to play dress-up, and this was no exception. I smiled back and continued walking clumsily in the garden and playing in the flowers. Knowing the Superwalk was only a few days away, I simply enjoyed that moment of solitude with nature and my mom before my next appearance in front of the crowd of many photographers and people.

The day of the Superwalk arrived. Our part in the event included a one-mile walk and then meeting the rest of the participants at the finish line. The itinerary for the other participants consisted of a twenty-mile walk. The Superwalk was quite an event for the March of Dimes, as it raised a significant amount of money for the organization. As I stood at the finish line in my shorts, Superwalk T-shirt, and poster-child banner from shoulder to hip, the walkers and runners smiled down at me as they crossed the line. My prosthesis showed, and the obvious scars on my hands stood out against the white and red lettering of my shirt.

It was a heartfelt moment as one of the participants picked me up and carried me with her as she ran, proudly displaying me as a reminder of what this fight against birth defects was all about. As she ran with me in her smooth steady pace, a feeling of love and gratitude flowed through me; I felt I could overcome any obstacle. Moments like these reinforced the idea that people were ultimately loving and compassionate—one of many such moments I would experience throughout my life.

Later that day, we had a call asking us to meet with Ed, the vice president of the national March of Dimes. He wanted to meet the family for dinner and give us an update on the status of my national poster child nomination.

Ed informed us over dinner that I had been selected as a finalist, out of 350 nominees. The final group now consisted of only four children, of which I was one. As Ed conducted an informal interview over dinner, photographers took several pictures of the family. Mom smiled as flashes from the camera lit up the dim room, but she could not help but ponder how well I would handle all of this publicity. She was concerned and had reservations about it, just as any loving mother would. She would lean on her faith and God again to get her through this experience. *It is out of my hands, and I trust the decision will be what we are supposed to do.* And with that thought, she squeezed me a little tighter as the photographers finished up the pictures.

As the March of Dimes headquarters was busy filtering the final four contestants, I remained busy with local appearances for various events. It was a time when we patiently awaited a decision but also knew I still had an important role to carry out as the local poster child. One of the events that stood out to me was an event called Wash Away Birth Defects. A catchy title indeed as the event was a car-washing fundraiser. After the car wash, there was a banquet held inside the building. One of the officials approached my mom.

"May, the main speaker is running late, and we were hoping you could step in and speak about your daughter and some of your personal experiences."

Mom tried to hide her look of hesitation but realized this was a good opportunity, and felt she may be able to help someone in the audience.

"I would be happy to," she stated.

As she took the podium, my mom explained to the audience what we had been through as a family. As I stood beside her through the speech, she gently reached down and took my hand into hers, a reassurance I needed at that moment. It was the first time I'd heard about the events of my life from my mom's point of view. A flood of tears filled my eyes, and I tried to hold it back. Waves of recognition washed over me as I listened to my mom speak about our past experiences together. I realized at that moment just how much my mom had been through in those six short years and how strong a person and mother she was. Just as she could never guess what it was like for me, I hadn't realized what an impact my life had on her.

As her beautiful speech was wrapping up, the audience stood and clapped for us. It was an amazing opportunity for my mom, and she hoped to have many more chances to speak on behalf of me and other children like me. It made the prospect of touring nationally all the more enticing.

The following day, Nancy from the national March of Dimes called and said they would like to meet with us to do a screen test with me. The screen test was set for a Thursday, and we were to arrive at the local March of Dimes office at 10:30. As Nancy, Ed, photographers, cameramen, and a multitude of other March of Dimes representatives arrived, I grew uneasy. Nancy immediately noticed the look of confusion on my face. Kneeling down beside me, she held me close to her. "Betsy, you are precious indeed, and today is very important. We are going to film you doing all sorts of things. The film and pictures are going to be viewed by national headquarters. We are doing this because of your nomination for national poster child. You are going to do great, and everyone here loves you, so I don't want you to be scared. Think of it as a play day … but with lots of pictures," she said with her reassuring smile.

As I looked down at my prosthesis showing from under my dress and the obvious scars on my hands, I became self-conscious about my physical imperfections being on film; however, I realized the importance of the events. I nodded as I sat on her knee and felt I was up to the challenge.

It was a long day, and the filming ended around eleven o'clock that night. It was now a waiting game, as the decision from National Headquarters would take a few days. It was a time of reflection and recording as my mom filled up pages of her journal quickly. She never expected to fill the pages of her journal as quickly as she had, but she did so knowing there was a message to be told somewhere within the retelling of my early years. How grateful she had been for that blank space in which to record her most personal feelings at times when she felt a need for expression. She soon realized those pages in her journal would continue to become filled as the March of Dimes president, Mr. Fike, called our house. Mom heard his voice on the conference call, as well as that of Nancy and another representative.

"Mrs. Burch, we have just seen the films of your daughter. They're beautiful, as is she," Mr. Fike stated.

"Thank you. I do hope we'll get a chance to see the films," Mom replied.

"Oh, you will. We have decided we want Betsy to be our national poster child for next year."

Mom had spent so much time hoping and expecting the best result, yet she didn't know what to say. Trying to remain calm, she gladly accepted the offer. Amazed, she told them that we would give 100 percent to the March of Dimes and were looking forward to a great year.

She realized in this instant that one chapter of my life, as well as hers, was closing and a new one was opening. I had always been special in her eyes. Now, we were fortunate enough to be able to go and share the spirit, courage, and triumph that I represented for her. We could show that having problems like mine need not handicap anyone.

11

Envisioning Success

As I started ascending the steady incline of the bridge, the muscles in my legs immediately felt the burn. As I continued the climb, Eric fell back a little behind me to take some additional photos of me running. I could feel the energy of those runners around me; we all had one goal in mind at that moment—making it to the top of the bridge. I dug in even harder, found that determination inside me, and kicked it into high gear. I knew I would need every last reserve of energy to make it to the top.

As I continued the climb, I remembered back to my year as national poster child. It was an amazing experience, just like this moment on the incline. I knew I would get to the top, no matter what. My goal was to run the entire race, without stopping to walk. The incline would be the first challenge to this goal of mine. As I felt my running blade adapt to the new incline, I kept my eyes on the top of the hill …

12

Into the Unknown

I remember things like the red carpet, the smiles from strangers, and the cameras. There were a handful of really nice people who stand out in my memories. There were at least a handful more that my mother got excited about, who I decided must be pretty important even though I didn't have a clue who they were. An example of this was Robert Redford. I took many of my cues from my mom. It was a testament to her strength and to the feelings of security that had been instilled in me that none of what happened that year phased me much.

At the end of 1979,

Me and Arnold Palmer on his golf course in Pennsylvania (Photo courtesy March of Dimes)

I had not yet been announced officially as the national poster child for March of Dimes, so the events that we did participate in were either with, or held for, the major supporters of the organization. The promotional photos and ad campaigns were getting underway, and every new event was an unexpected opportunity. By that time, the March of Dimes was focused on providing education and outreach, mostly targeted toward women and mothers, to help prevent and treat birth defects. They had made great strides, just as they once had with their original mission to prevent polio. Around the time that I was poster child, their campaigns relied heavily on working together with celebrities, stores, and public figures to generate awareness. It was the glitziest and most glamorous time to be involved with the March of Dimes, and their fashion shows, galas, and celebrity endorsements were going a long way toward drawing donations. My year as a national poster child was a wild adventure. It was formative and life-changing, but for me it was just the way things were.

At the end of the summer, my mom and I were flown by the March of Dimes to Pennsylvania. It was the first of many trips, and this one in particular was important as we were filming a video with Arnold Palmer to promote my upcoming role. Although I was unsure who he was, my mom did her best to explain his position. As a child, I was seldom excited about the stardom of others but rather took it all in stride.

After landing safely in Pittsburg, we were greeted by Ed, who was a representative of the March of Dimes. He had a staff with him that included a secretary named Ronnie and a photographer named John. We had met Ed previously in Atlanta at various fundraisers earlier that year. Ed was excited to see me again, and I was always thrilled to meet people I recognized. The next thing we knew, we were heading off to Latrobe, Pennsylvania, to meet Arnold Palmer. We made a quick stop at the hotel to change clothes before heading to the greens. It was at this point my mom realized she had misjudged the weather here.

"It feels unusually cold here ... it's still blazing hot in Atlanta," my mom said in the car, hoping for some reassurance from Ed.

"Apparently, it's unseasonably cold here at the moment, breaking all kinds of weather records. The high temp today is only going to be thirty-eight degrees."

As Ed said this, I could see the worry on Mom's face. We were both dressed in skirts and short-sleeves, according to the fact that it was still summer in most of the United States.

We arrived at the hotel, and Ed reminded us that we were running a little behind schedule and to meet back in the lobby as soon as we were ready. Once in the room, I quickly unloaded all of my clothes into a drawer. For a one-night stay, the amount of clothing we brought was a bit excessive, but the March of Dimes always told us to pack several outfits, and then they would pick out one or two things for me to wear in the photo shoots. My mom looked over my shoulder as I unpacked, but there was not a single piece of outerwear to be found in our arsenal of clothing and no time to buy any.

"Betsy, I'm sorry I didn't bring anything warmer to wear. We'll stop by a store after the photo shoot today, and I'll get us some jackets," Mom said as she helped me get my dress on.

"It's okay," I said, trying to reassure her.

We met Ed back in the lobby, and we were on our way to Arnold Palmer's golf course. Mom explained to me that Arnold Palmer was one of golf's most prolific champions, and he was also a prominent spokesman for the March of Dimes. A trustee of the organization, he would be part of the ad campaign that would eventually be run when I was officially announced as the 1980 national poster child. Until that time, we had a lot of promotional stepping-stones to cross, this one being the first.

As I listened to Mom describe the upcoming shoot, I did my best to process this information, just as any other six-year-old would do.

Upon arrival at Arnold Palmer's golf course, I noticed no one else was there. The camera crew we'd met just a few hours earlier was now running late. It was freezing out, and as the wind blew across the open greens, I cuddled close to my mom in search of some warmth. Soon, three station wagons pulled up carrying the photographers and their equipment.

"Betsy, we are going to have you head to the ninth tee for some photos," one of the photographers said. "We have some junior golf clubs for you. Let's go practice a bit before Mr. Palmer gets here."

I nodded and headed out to the ninth tee, following all the photographers. Mom trailed behind us since she could see I felt comfortable taking the lead.

As I was playing and posing with the golf clubs, I noticed a gentleman walking toward us. I stopped my playful activity. I watched as this very calm yet apparently prominent man headed toward me. I could see he was carrying a golf club in his hand. He was dressed in a nice pair of slacks and wore a blue sweater over his shirt, which was neatly tucked into his slacks. I noticed his white belt and matching white golf shoes, as they contrasted on the green grass. He had a few people with him, carrying his remaining clubs and other items. As

(Photo courtesy March of Dimes)

he approached, he squatted down beside me.

"You must be Betsy," he said.

I nodded, shyness sweeping over me.

"Those are some nice golf clubs you have. Let's try and hit the golf ball together a little bit," he said.

His conversation was kind, his voice gentle. I became more comfortable with him. He looked at my leg and hands with admiration, and I felt a warm energy coming from him. Children can be quite intuitive, and this would be the first of many people I would learn to read. Like many of the people we would meet, I had no idea who he was, but I was interested in the aura of importance he gave off. The photographers took many pictures of us together; however, we had to finish the shoot early as the weather was not cooperating. We rescheduled for the following day to finish up the photo shoot.

As we headed back to the hotel, we finally had time to stop at a shopping mall to buy some sweaters and jackets. Having my mind set on swimming once we were back at the hotel pool, I reminded my mom how much I hated shopping and begged her to hurry. She knew I loved to swim, but she was less than enthusiastic about getting in a pool, especially after spending the day freezing outside on the golf course.

"Betsy, we will see about swimming. Right now I need to find us some warmer clothes for tomorrow."

I could hear the persistence in her voice and decided to follow her instructions.

We found warmer clothes to get us through the following day and finally found our way back to the hotel. Hungry and cold, the warmth of the hotel lobby and restaurant was very comforting to my mom and me. We were alone again in the hotel, and as we ate dinner, we were happy to be together. We reflected on the day, and she said how proud she was of me.

"Are you ready to go swimming now?" Mom asked as we were sitting after dinner.

I looked at her with my big brown eyes and a huge smile on

my face. I thought back to the conversation between her and me at the mall just a short time ago. I had accepted the fact that the pool was probably not happening tonight. It was a pleasant surprise from my mom. She was good at surprising me.

As we were leaving the restaurant, she stopped by the front desk to ask about the pool.

"It is an indoor pool and also heated, ma'am," the hotel clerk told her.

I could see relief in Mom's eyes.

In the hotel room, we put on our bathing suits and found our way to the water. I had become an avid swimmer in the last months since I started taking lessons at the Georgia State Recreation pool.

I always found happiness in swimming.
Photo courtesy March of Dimes

"Betsy, you're like a fish in water," she laughed as I dove headfirst into the pool and began swimming side to side.

I was perfectly content in my underwater world. I was swimming, and I loved it. My ability to swim meant so much to my mom, and she was always amazed whenever I displayed any natural ability. As she continued to watch me swim, she thought to herself that it was only six years ago she'd feared that I might not walk. Now look at her little girl, swimming like any other child. It was a moment where Mom felt again that her faith had brought her to this place. She could feel her dad's loving presence next to her. She knew he was not only proud of his granddaughter but proud of his daughter as well.

When we returned to the hotel room late after swimming, it was difficult to fall asleep, despite our busy day. The pillows were hard, and we both tossed and turned. I didn't remind her then, but I had asked Mom before we left home if I could bring my pillow with us. She'd said no, as it was just one more thing to pack, and we had little enough room as it was. As I lay in bed, I wondered if she wished she had listened to me. I thought to myself there would be a learning curve to this whole frequent travel business. As I lay there remembering the events of the day and finding comfort in my mom next to me, I drifted off to a peaceful sleep.

From the moment we got up the following morning, it was easy to see that it was going to be a beautiful day. The weather was much improved, and the drive back out to the golf course was magnificent. There were green hills upon green hills, waves of them like waves in the ocean. As the sun shone down on them from the blue sky above, they reflected a radiating beauty.

We met again at the ninth tee, and Arnold Palmer was already there when we arrived. The cameramen and photographers had their equipment set up and were prepared to film the ad for a TV spot. Mr. Palmer and I both had a script to recite, and I was able to memorize and deliver it on the first take. There were many people from the local March of Dimes chapter there. They were very encouraging, each in his or her own way, and gave my mom peace of mind that I would tolerate this process well and would meet it with unconditional acceptance. It turned out they were right.

Near the end of the filming and photo shoot, Mom could not resist getting her photo taken with Mr. Palmer as well. We both gave a nod of approval as she posed for the photo. I saw a childlike energy coming from my mom, and it made me smile.

We had successfully completed our tour in Pennsylvania and headed back to the airport where we waited to board the plane in the Red Carpet Room. *Another perk of being an important traveler,* I thought to myself. As I sat there with Mom, I recalled the rough landing of the plane just the day before. This would be only my second time on an airplane. Mom must have seen the scared look on my face.

"What's wrong, Betsy?" she asked.

As I sat there holding my doll in my lap, I stumbled with the words. "I'm scared of the airplane."

Mom remembered the turbulent landing of the day before and realized it had an impact on me that she hadn't noticed before. She did her best to calm me.

"Turbulence is normal," she said in an overly confident voice. "We just never know where the turbulence might be. But the pilots are trained to deal with that sort of thing, and they are very good."

I took some reassurance from her words but also wondered if she believed herself completely. I thought she might have been trying to emotionally prepare herself for another bumpy ride. Either way, it was the first of many plane rides to come, and it was clear that we were in for a lot of highs and lows in all aspects of travel and life on the road.

Me and Colonel Sanders, Atlanta, Georgia.
(Photo courtesy March of Dimes)

We continued to attend local events in Atlanta through the fall and winter months, making appearances for the March of Dimes. My job was to create awareness and to help raise money for the charity. As summer approached, we received word from the March of Dimes that our next venue would include a picnic at Piedmont Park in Atlanta, and the guest of honor would be Colonel Sanders. He was a chairman of the March of Dimes organization. As we arrived at the park, quite a crowd was gathering for the picnic. Many of the members of the crowd were reporters.

I sat next to Colonel Sanders, and there were many pictures made with him. As a child, I was unsure who this elderly gentleman was, and I began to feel a bit uneasy around him. He apparently had a granddaughter who was born with birth defects, and he was very loving with all of the kids there, each with their various disabilities. Years later, my mom told me he picked up my hands and kissed each one, a gesture I don't remember personally but one that seemed to have a profound impact on those around us.

The day in the park was drawing to a close—another successful event and fundraiser for the March of Dimes.

"If it's all right, we would like to come back to the house with you and film some pictures of Betsy," a photographer said to my mom.

She thought about it for a moment. "That would be just fine."

As she said this, she was reminded that the role of national poster child included times of spontaneity and picture taking at any given moment.

Of course, as an innocent child, I was thrilled by this and assumed that if this was what being a poster child meant, I was going to be great at it. The crew came back to our home and took various pictures of me jumping on the trampoline and skating around the house.

Days continued to be filled with blurbs and articles about me in the local papers. My mom showed me these, along with an equal amount of mail that arrived for us, most of it from the March of Dimes containing photos and letters from the people we'd met already in that short precursor to an eventful year.

Friends and acquaintances at church clipped articles for us and told me how much they enjoyed following my journey. For my mom, this meant that before long her scrapbooking duties would threaten to become a full-time job.

Between the photo sessions, my mom enjoyed the days of normalcy where she could take her kids to the pool. We would go to the neighborhood pool whenever we had an opportunity. My mom had placed me in swim lessons a few years earlier, even before I could remember, and I flourished in learning how to swim. Of course, even at this young age, the challenge of swimming with a deficient lower extremity had its challenges, but I was determined to overcome them. Later in life, my willingness to adapt would take me to great heights as a swimmer.

"I can't get enough of seeing your confidence in the water, Betsy," Mom said.

She took a break to film me for a short time, and when she got back into the water, she said, "You're becoming such a wonderful swimmer."

"Yeah, I'm pretty good at soccer too."

She laughed. She was more thankful than she could say for my outlook on life. It inspired her. But the truth is I may not have had that outlook if it had not been for the way I was raised. I had no shortage of confidence.

It wasn't long after getting home from the pool the phone was rang, and it was Nancy, our national March of Dimes liaison. I was in the living room, and I heard Mom talking on the phone to her.

"Yes!" my mom shouted from the next room. I heard her hang up the phone, and she came running into the den.

"Betsy, we are going to Utah to meet Robert Redford!" she said with excitement. She picked me up and twirled me around in her arms. I was all smiles and laughter, radiating the energy my mom was beaming down on me.

"We have so much to do to get ready," she exclaimed, walking out of the living room as I sat on the floor and played with my dolls. I thought to myself, *Who is Robert Redford?* And then the importance of my dolls took precedence.

As I was busy playing in the living room of our house, my mom was busy making phone calls; I heard her on the phone with a friend.

"We are leaving Sunday for Salt Lake City to meet Robert Redford!" She was as giddy as a young girl. "And we will likely meet the Osmonds and possibly Willie Nelson."

Oh, the Osmonds, I thought to myself. *I like them, Donnie and Marie. I like Donnie's purple outfits. That might be fun. I like the* Donnie and Marie Show. *But who is this Robert Redford guy anyway?*

I never understood, until I was much older, my mom's eagerness or why all of her girlfriends exclaimed, in the following days, how jealous they were and how much they wanted to go with us.

As it happened, the event was delayed until the following week. As big as the March of Dimes was at that time and with so many important schedules to consider, it was only natural for some hiccups to occur. My mom was hardly daunted by this. She was a ball of energy on our flight out to Utah, and seeing her so excited calmed my nerves over flying. The headphones, breakfast, and first-class treatment from the flight attendants did the rest.

Our connecting flight was with American Airlines, and Nancy joined us at the airport. I was excited to see her and sit with her. On the plane, we ate and drank the whole time, and Mom met and talked with a lady from Salt Lake City while I talked and played with Nancy.

Once we arrived, our busy schedule started immediately. We met and took photographs with Wendy of Wendy's restaurants. It was terribly hot outside, and as we drove to the hotel, we took in the beautiful view of desert giving way to gorgeous mountains. We checked in at the Salt Lake City Hilton and headed to our room.

"We're on the eighth floor, Betsy," Mom said. She always let me push the elevator button.

I eagerly pressed the number eight, and we were on our way. When we arrived in our room, I headed to the curtains and opened them.

"Look, Mom, you can see all the beautiful mountains!"

As my mom stared out the window, she smiled at the view as if the peacefulness of the mountains gave her renewed hope and reminded her that through all struggles there is also beauty.

"Yes they are quite amazing," she said. "Now, we're meeting Nancy in a few minutes, so let's get dressed for dinner."

I quickly changed into a dress Mom had packed for me, and we headed downstairs to meet Nancy. Nancy was a very beautiful woman with long brown hair. Her eyes were as blue as the sky, and she was tall and slender, and her figure quite modelesque. She always dressed nicely and carried herself with much grace and elegance. I adored her not only for her outer beauty but for her undeniable beauty within. A lasting bond formed between Nancy and me but also between Nancy and my mom. Nancy would become the calm presence on many occasions in the future when a tired and cranky six-year-old had had enough. Over the coming months, through exhausting schedules, mass pictures, many airline flights, late hours, and God knows how many telethons, Nancy would be the one that held it all—held *us* all—together. My mom could not have possibly done it alone, and Nancy was there for both of us.

After dinner, I couldn't help but ask Mom about the hotel pool. I had quite a love for them.

"Mom, can I go swimming?"

"Of course you can," she said, and our smiles were reciprocated.

As Nancy and Mom sat at the side of the pool and watched me, I went into my own underwater world. When I submerged myself underwater and began swimming, my thoughts of being physically different melted away. I was renewed, like the dawn of a new day, and realized I could go on through anything.

After swimming, we said goodnight to Nancy and headed to our hotel room. Nancy had gone over the itinerary for the following day with Mom as they sat by the pool. Seeing that it was a busy one, Mom settled me in bed and called her sister, Adele. As I was drifting to sleep, I could hear some of their conversation about us possibly going to visit after we were finished with our assignment in Salt Lake City. Adele and her family had a summer home in Jackson Hole, Wyoming, and they were currently there.

"Let me check on tickets tomorrow. We could just fly from Utah to Wyoming for a few days before heading back home," Mom said.

I would love to see my cousins … And with that thought, I was off to dreamland.

It was morning, and my mom was stirring in the room. As she opened the curtains, she said, "Time to rise and shine, Betsy."

I could feel an unusual excitement radiating from my mom. We were scheduled to meet Robert Redford today. As I turned to the light coming in the window, I saw the haze over the mountains.

"Mom, those mountains aren't even awake yet."

It was early—earlier than usual—but mom was already dressed and ready to go. I wiped the sleep from my eyes and gently placed my prosthetic leg on. I never slept with it on as it was quite cumbersome and, to some extent, uncomfortable. As I stood up and finished buckling the straps of my prosthesis, I headed for the closet where my dresses were neatly hanging.

"What dress should I wear, Mom?" I knew this day had some importance for my mom, and I wanted to look nice.

"Let's see …" She started to go through the hangers. She stopped at a blue dress with a white top covered in flowers.

"This one looks perfect."

I was reluctant to disagree, and with a smile I took the dress and got dressed. As I was putting my dress on, Mom laid out my little white socks; they were anklet socks with ribbons around the top. They would go well with my Mary Jane shoes. My dresses always fell above my knees; this way people could see my leg and the obvious prosthesis I was wearing.

We made our way down to the lobby of the hotel where Nancy and a man named David were waiting for us. David was a representative from the Provo, Utah, chapter of the March of Dimes. As we stopped by David's office for an updated itinerary of the events of the day, there was a sign on the wall that read, *Welcome, Betsy and Mom!*

It was the little things like this that truly delighted me.

"The Osmonds had a prior engagement and will not be able to meet with us today," David stated.

I'm pretty sure the disappointment showed on my face.

"Betsy, we can still tour their dressing rooms. You can see where they get their hair and makeup done, and we can look around their studio a bit. Would you like that?"

This appeased me somewhat, and I agreed to the plan. He went on to tell us we would be driving up to Sundance Mountain Resort to meet Robert Redford around four that afternoon. As we left the office, I looked in the distance and noticed how the town was beautifully surrounded by mountains. Even as a child, I regarded the mountains as sacred, as they held many secrets of the past. They observed peoples from times before me in their struggles and saw how they overcame them, just as they were watching me overcome struggles of my own.

As we were driving to the Osmonds' studio, we stopped for lunch at the Four Winds Restaurant. As a six-year-old, I had a love for hot dogs, and these were not always easy to come by in some of the fancier restaurants we frequented. This was the case at the Four Winds as well. Mom and Nancy were always trying to find food that would appease me. I would be offered some of the most expensive meals possible, yet hot dogs or mac 'n' cheese were always a hit; I was a typical kid at heart.

As lunch was drawing to a close, I started to get impatient about leaving.

"When are we going to the Osmonds' studio?" I inquired to Nancy.

"It won't be much longer. Let's walk around outside while the others finish their lunch."

She always seemed to know what to do in my moments of impatience. I think she realized how much this role could affect a child, how it could mean having to grow up much faster than most children my age. She wanted me to have this opportunity, but she also wanted me to be able to experience normal kid stuff as well. I always felt she had my best interests in mind, and I therefore listened to her and let her take me under her wing. It was a special relationship indeed.

The drive to the Osmond studio was relatively quick, and I was glad. Once there, I looked inside their dressing room and sat in their makeup chairs. Although I was upset I would not be meeting them in person, I concluded that this was the next best option.

Me and Robert Redford on photo shoot at Sundance Mountain Resort
(Photo courtesy March of Dimes)

"Betsy?" I heard my name as I was pretending to be a star in the makeup chair. "We need to wrap things up here and head for Sundance to meet Robert Redford," David said.

Brought back to reality, I agreed and hopped out of the chair.

The drive to Sundance Mountain Resort lasted a bit longer than the one from the restaurant to the Osmonds' studio. In the car, I could see and feel a childlike energy radiating from Mom. I was still unaware of who I was about to meet, but to my mom, it seemed very important.

After we arrived at Sundance, we sat in a room in a small building awaiting the arrival of Robert Redford. I noticed the simplicity of my surroundings; there were a few chairs in this room and a desk with a large window looking out unto the rolling fields in between the mountains. The room felt very earthy, and I found comfort in it. I noticed a red car pull up outside, and a slender man emerged from the driver's side. He had a sleek physique and held himself with a peaceful yet serious aura. He was wearing blue jeans with a blue and white checkered shirt that contrasted his eyes. His worn, brown leather cowboy boots complemented his feathery blond hair and tan face. I felt this man was of some importance, and I appreciated the energy he gave off.

Everyone stopped what they were doing the moment he walked in. As soon as he entered, it was as if he was the only

Me and Robert Redford photo shoot on Sundance Mountain Resort (Photo courtesy March of Dimes)

person in the room. I would come to find out later the room we were in was his office.

"Hi, Betsy. I understand you don't know who I am," he stated as he kneeled down to me and reached out to shake my hand. The perceived importance of him brought out the shyness within me, and all I could do at that moment was smile and nod. He reciprocated the smile and then stood to meet the others in the room. Although not necessary, he turned and introduced himself to everyone else.

Earlier that day, in David's office, we had been informed that the plan was to have my photos taken with Robert Redford on horses. It was another promotion for the March of Dimes where local people in the area would ride their horses to raise money for the charity. It was termed Ride-a-Thon, a spinoff of the walk-a-thon, which was what the March of Dimes was best known for. As I was placed on my designated horse, an Arabian stallion, I was filled with thrill and excitement. From an early age, I developed a deep love for all animals, and this horse was no different.

As I sat there on my horse while Robert was getting on his, mine became spooked and started to become quite skittish. The look of fear on my face must have been evident as Robert quickly climbed off his horse and grabbed me in one fell swoop. In an instant, I felt safe again in the arms of Robert Redford; if I had only known the significance of this! From that moment on, Robert was in charge of how the photo shoot was going to be carried out. He made it clear I was not to get on a horse without him, and none of the photographers contested his request. Given the confidence and polite sternness he presented, only a fool would have defied him.

"Such a pretty dress for a pretty girl," he said to me. I responded with smiles and friendly conversation as the photographers worked diligently, capturing our emotion and poses together. The end result was multiple photos of him holding me on his horse, and as I looked to my mom standing on the ground a few feet away, her smile was from ear to ear.

Mom looks so pretty, I thought to myself. She was, in reality, a very pretty woman with light brown hair and green eyes. Her hair, short and wispy, brought out her inner child and revealed her beauty. She was wearing a short-sleeved, dainty blouse, a rose-colored skirt, and high-heeled sandals. Her perfect little painted toes accented the opening of her sandals. She would later tell me how indescribable this experience was for her and how Robert Redford was every bit as handsome as he was in pictures. I enjoyed the experience and would grow to appreciate it even more when I was able to recognize his fame later in life.

The drive back down the mountain had many winding passes. I was reflecting on the busy day, and as I was listening to David, Nancy, and Mom talk about the March of Dimes, my eyes grew heavy. I laid my head on Mom's shoulder and drifted off to sleep.

"Betsy, we're here."

I opened my eyes and realized I'd slept the entire ride back to the hotel. We were all staying at the same hotel, and after such a busy day, we welcomed the hotel restaurant for dinner. Feeling a bit rejuvenated after dinner, I of course asked to go swimming. My love for swimming was one thing, but I was enamored by all of the different hotel pools. David, his family, Nancy, and Mom went swimming with me, and I enjoyed this part of the day very much. Although I could have swum for hours, Mom was getting tired, and it was time to call an end to a wonderful day. When we returned to the hotel room, Mom called her sister, Adele, to tell her about the events of the day.

"We are going to see your aunt Del tomorrow in Wyoming," she told me after hanging up the phone.

I was excited, as I was very close to my aunt and my cousins. It was a perfect ending to a perfect day. The following day, we went by the Mormon temple and then caught a short flight to Idaho Falls. As I looked out the airplane window, noticing the

Great Salt Lake below, I appreciated its vastness. All the while, Mom sat beside me sipping champagne. *Another perk of an important traveler,* I thought.

We were met at the airport by Aunt Del, Gran, and my cousins. We were all smiles, and I appreciated some normalcy of life at the moment. No cameras or photographers. I could just be myself and be a kid for a little bit. The ninety-mile drive to their summer home in Jackson Hole went by fast as I was busy playing with my cousins in the back of the car. The days that followed included activities with my family in the mountains of Wyoming. I remember the beautiful scenery filled with lakes, wildflowers, wild animals, cool nights under blankets outside on the porch, and picnics during the days on the side of the mountains.

We headed home a few days later and were met by my dad and siblings. It felt nice being back home, and I reminisced on the previous days with childlike gratitude.

13
Holding Strong

As I continued my focus on the top of the hill, I remembered back to when Eric and I first started training for this run some nine months ago. In November, Eric and I had done a small 5K in Charleston as a trial. I had built up to almost three miles a day by that point, and the run was intended to give me a good idea of what to expect on the Bridge Run, being half its distance. The 5K was a Turkey Run, held on Thanksgiving Day. I ended the race with a time of forty-two minutes—a huge accomplishment for me!

The running blade arrived just after the beginning of the year, and I was excited to try it. But I immediately realized that running with a new leg, however dynamic it may be, was going to set me back in my training. The carbon fiber foot was light and springy compared to the leg I was used to. Impossible to walk on because it only consisted of a forefoot, the blade could only be used for running, which meant I had to relearn the mechanics of that one activity and had a limited amount of time each day to do so. It was a period of trial and error, and several trips to the prosthetist's office, before I felt comfortable in the appendage.

Eric and I ran just about every day for seven months. We finally accomplished a six-mile run only a week before the April

Bridge Run. Our last trial run that week was on the course itself, and I was able to do it without stopping. From that point, it was just a matter of holding strong until race day.

The top of the bridge seemed so far away still. I thought it strange to look down to the street and see the yellow lines of the road. Here I was running on top of them, when in usual circumstances, the lines are used to navigate drivers inside their lane. They had a different purpose today. For every line I crossed, I was closer to the top of the bridge and ultimately closer to the finish. I thought back to the days of my youth, and memories suddenly filled my mind.

14
The Tour Continues

As September slipped into Atlanta, the first hints of fall were in the air. The humidity had broken somewhat, and nights were growing cooler. As the seasons changed, I was also transitioning into my new life as national poster child. Change was nothing new to me. With so many surgeries behind me, I was adapting to my physical challenges. I knew there would be more surgeries in my future but at a slower pace now. Most of the major procedures had been completed.

In between promotional pictures for the March of Dimes with the heads of local and national corporations and business chains, there were visits to Dr. King, my orthopedic physician and miracle worker for my right leg. I had a follow-up appointment with him one September morning.

As I sat on the exam table awaiting his arrival, Mom sat patiently in the chair by the window reading a magazine. I never really enjoyed sitting in the exam rooms, waiting on one doctor or another to arrive. The bland-colored walls, the crinkly paper on the examination table, and orthopedic equipment all around—the rooms were all the same. I felt lonely sitting there, and this gave rise to feelings of solitude and anxiety. While I looked around at the four dimly painted walls, I couldn't help but ponder, even as a child, what the doctor may or may not say. *Am I doing okay? Is he going to say I need another operation? Will I have to do X-rays today?* The exam table was a place of reflection for me, on what I had been through and what was to still come.

As I sat there, my thoughts were interrupted by movement outside the door. I knew the sound of Dr. King getting my chart out of the chart holder on the outside of the door. The noise was followed by a silent pause and then the sound of the door opening.

Dr. King was a very nice man with a stern bedside manner, a straight shooter. He did not engage in casual conversation and was very factual in his demeanor. Always garbed in a white lab coat, he had once intimidated me. But I was no longer afraid of him. I rather appreciated the intelligent aura he gave off. I had become comfortable with the white lab coat and his direct demeanor. Through his dedication and the success of my surgeries, my trust in him was complete.

As he stood in the room before us, I listened intently to Dr. King's words and did my best to understand his statements. Mom usually did most of the talking for both of us. Dr. King was a person we rarely questioned in his medical decisions and advice for me.

"Betsy, you are doing well, and your growth and development after all of your surgeries look great," he said as he pulled the rolling chair closer to the table where I was sitting.

This was my cue to remove my heavy prosthesis so he could examine the work he had done on my leg. As I removed the prosthetic and socks covering my short leg, he gently placed his hand on it. He examined my leg with much focus and admiration, just as an artist or sculptor admires their most recent work of art.

"No X-rays today, but I want to see you in six months, and we'll do X-rays at that time," he said.

I breathed a sigh of relief. I dreaded having X-rays. The cold metal tables with even colder and harder X-ray plates placed under my extremities were unpleasant to say the least. While Dr. King and my mom talked a bit more about my progress and future plans, I placed my heavy and bulky prosthesis back on. Dr. King's smile of approval as he turned to leave the room only added more reassurance that I was doing well indeed.

From Dr. King's office, we went by my elementary school. Registration for the new school year was upon us. Between all of our upcoming travels and unpredictable schedule, it would be an interesting school year. My mom was a teacher by trade and was certified to teach me while we were on the road. She talked to the principal and to the first-grade teacher, and they were supportive of my modified schedule over the upcoming school year. This would not have been possible if it were not for the love and support of my first-grade teacher, Ms. Bryant. She was a lovely woman, with white hair and a very gentle demeanor.

As Ms. Bryant and my mom spoke of the itinerary for the upcoming year, other kids and parents were trickling into the room. I became a little fearful for the first time in many months, pondering how the other kids would accept me. I stepped a little closer to Mom and took her hand. As I did this, another girl, named Amanda, with an obvious birthmark on her face entered the room with her mother. I was not relieved by this, but it gave me hope that I would not be the only one with a physical difference. This common bond between me and Amanda made it tolerable and hopeful for us both; we were not alone. Our eyes met with a look of understanding and compassion for each other.

Mom told me later that it was no coincidence we were in the same class. "God puts people in our path for a reason, Betsy."

She also told me later how it warmed her heart to see Amanda, and she was hopeful that Amanda and I would find ease from any self-consciousness we might experience. Looking back, I feel we were meant to be together to help each other and be strong— and we were. Amanda and I were friends throughout our entire elementary school years together, and there were many days we simply helped each other by being around one another. We are still friends today.

School started, and I did very well settling into the routine of school life. I knew I had upcoming travels and appreciated the normalcy of attending school while I was not traveling. I was an eager learner and had the desire to succeed not only in my personal life but in my academic life as well. I made friends easily and felt an overall acceptance from everyone around me.

As the end of the month approached, Ms. Bryant asked me one afternoon to share my schedule for the upcoming events with the March of Dimes to the class. I spoke freely and confidently about my role as poster child and informed my classmates of my schedule. They were eager to hear about my travels, as they knew I would return with interesting show-and-tell topics.

I could not have asked for a better support system from my classmates. I was very fortunate to be surrounded with love and without any bullying or feelings of intimidation. It was a time of innocence for us kids, and we were allowed to enjoy it. Much of that appears to be lost in present-day school systems.

As this particular school day ended, I said my temporary good-byes to my classmates and Ms. Bryant. I would be gone for about seven days on my upcoming trip to New York. It was a trip to the Women's World Tennis Association Awards Dinner. In addition to my own attendance, the March of Dimes wanted both my mom and dad to attend. It took some planning on my parents' part since Dad travelled with his job and my siblings could not miss school. Mom arranged for my sister and brother to stay with family friends at home so they could keep up their school attendance. And before I knew it, we were off to New York.

As the plane approached La Guardia, I didn't even flinch. I was becoming quite accustomed to flying. It was a big change from that first flight to Pennsylvania a few months before. In a short time, I had embraced my job as national poster child, and flying just became part of the process.

I was happy to see Nancy at the gate when we stepped off the flight. It was a warm welcome between us since it had been a few weeks since I'd last seen her. Mom was always glad to see Nancy as well because she was a breath of fresh air and such a positive supporter of not only my role as poster child but of the organization as well.

Of course we took a cab downtown, and as I stared through the windows, I felt as if I were in another world. The city was crowded, and I gazed at the buildings densely packed in side by side. There were oceans of concrete streets and buildings as far as the eye could see. The cab ride was typical of a New York experience; tearing through the city as buildings flew by. When we finally arrived at our hotel, I noticed an old brick building with a sign above the door that read *Plaza Park Hotel*. In my six-year-old mind, the building looked massive.

Inside, I eagerly pressed the elevator button as I always did and started counting the floors, "Ten … twenty … thirty …"

Mom placed her hand on my shoulder, and I knew it was a reminder to keep the floor counting to myself. Considering Dad was getting increasingly uncomfortable the higher we went, as he was not much for heights, or elevators, I continued the count silently in my head. As we entered our hotel room, I noticed a glass chandelier and luxurious drapes. I felt like a princess in a castle.

"Betsy, we are scheduled to have dinner with Nancy at the World Trade Center, so we need to get changed into our dresses," Mom said, and in an instant I was brought back to reality and out of my sky-high dreams.

I quickly changed into one of the dresses Mom had packed for me. I took one last glance at the chandelier as we were leaving the hotel room. We were off on another wild cab ride to the World Trade Center.

As we entered the elevator, Mom pressed 107, which was the highest of all the numbers. I knew from the previous elevator ride in the hotel not to count floors aloud, as Dad was looking even queasier. I stood there quietly and held in my childish excitement as the extremely fast elevator rose to the restaurant on the top level.

Nancy had a table picked out with a direct view of the Empire State Building and, just beyond, the Statue of Liberty. It was an awe-inspiring view. I would not truly appreciate this moment until later in life. Dusk was approaching, and the sun was setting over the city; we watched as the lights turned on throughout the city. It was gorgeous, all of it, from the green-lit bridges and the city outside to the real, plush towels in the restaurant bathroom inside.

We rode the subway back to the hotel, and this included a glimpse into another side of the city. There were so many poor and desolate people riding the subway. One man in particular had on several pairs of pants and shirts, which looked to be the entirety of his worldly possessions. This was a new world to me. I wanted to help those people I was on the subway with but was frightened at the same time. I felt the comfort and safety of my parents beside me, and I was glad when we arrived at our stop.

The subway stop was right by the plaza, and the sidewalks were still swarming with people, and taxis were still busily clogging the streets as we ascended once more to our room. The rest of the evening was uneventful, and we turned in early as we knew the following day would start early and be a long day of publicity and pictures.

The thing I would learn about hotels that baffled me was that sometimes they offered lavish breakfasts, and other times they offered nothing at all. We never quite knew what to expect. There was a delicious spread on this particular morning, and after indulging in it, we walked a block to the Ritz Hotel. This is where the meeting of the Women's Tennis Association was being held and where I was scheduled to make an appearance.

As we sat in a small room with representatives from the March of Dimes, Martina Navratilova walked in, and I immediately recognized her from the tennis match we attended the previous year. She came over and knelt down by me, and we started talking as if we were old friends. She took my hand, and we walked into the next room. The room was large and filled with many people. Martina was making a speech at the conference on this day, and my part was to be introduced by her.

After she introduced me, she and I exchanged a few words into the microphone, and then she sat me down in the chair next to the podium. I sat quietly as she finished her speech, which emphasized her support of the March of Dimes organization.

As the Women's Tennis Association Event was finishing, mid-afternoon approached. It was the middle of the day in New York, and the streets were filled with people everywhere. I marveled at this, and to my mind it was like being in a maze in a carnival. Block after block, we encountered a never-ending flow of people and buildings as we walked the rivers of concrete walkways. I stuck close to my parents, never letting go of my mom's hand. This was our free time before a dinner gala later that evening.

I finally got my wish to have a hot dog while I was travelling on the road as poster child. My mom stopped at the first Nathan's hot dog stand on a corner, and in a New York minute, I was a happy kid eating a hot dog for lunch.

We continued our walk back to the hotel to rest a little while before getting ready for the dinner that evening. As night approached, my mom started to get me dressed. Mom always worried over my hair a little bit; I guess she wanted to make sure I looked good for the mass pictures scheduled for me. It was the life of a star, and I did not even realize it at the time.

"That hair ..." she mumbled. "I really must get something done with it," Mom stated as she rolled my fine hair into rollers. I just sat there and let her do it, otherwise knowing it might cause her much distress.

As I finished putting my dress on, I looked over at my dad

and noticed his tuxedo. *He looks fancy,* I thought to myself. I don't think I had ever seen Dad dressed in a tuxedo before. As my eyes left him and looked over to Mom, I noticed her beautiful cranberry-colored dress with its small matching jacket. My orange and white fluffy dress, black patent-leather shoes, and dressy barrettes in my hair complemented my parents' outfits nicely. I twirled about the room endlessly, and as I looked up to see the beautiful chandelier, I was the princess in her castle again.

We met Nancy in the lobby, and her beauty was radiant. She was wearing a black lace-up dress with matching black high-heel shoes. We headed down to the grand ballroom where we were immediately met by representatives from the New York chapter of the March of Dimes. The grand ballroom was beautiful, and a wonderful band was playing. This was a huge event, and there were many television and movie stars all around me. It was my first experience at a gala, and I was a little confused by the fact that the dinner courses were served sporadically between dances.

The press was all over the place, and pictures were constantly being taken. Before we got too far into the dinner and dancing, the March of Dimes public relations person came to claim us and steered us over to David Hartman's table. He picked me up and sat me on his knee. Pictures were taken, and he danced with me to "You Light up My Life." It was a moment we would discuss later on an episode of *Good Morning America.* As the gala went on, various photo opportunities arose. A picture was taken of me with Eileen Fulton. She was a famous actress on *As the World Turns.* I became instant friends with her, and fate would have it that she had been the narrator of the small film the March of Dimes made of me a few months earlier.

Before the night came to an end, I was announced to the crowd as the 1980 March of Dimes national poster child. I was presented with a basket of fresh flowers, and as I stood on the stage, I beamed with pride and excitement.

It was a whirlwind night, and as I fell asleep that night in the comfort of the hotel room, I felt surrounded by love, peace, and security and gave thanks for the day's events. Even as a child, knowing I was physically different from others, I was given an incredible opportunity, and I gladly accepted it with gratitude and grace. It was an opportunity that, although it made me grow up faster than most, gave me the courage and strength to face adversity head on. It allowed me to reach down deep into my being and know that being different was not only okay but part of what made me special.

The following morning, we packed our things. Our trip and appearance in New York was coming to an end. We took a taxi to La Guardia Airport and parted ways with my dad, as he had to fly to Chicago on business. It was something my mom and I were becoming used to, taking many flights together.

We were a little early for our flight, so we waited in the VIP room at the airport. Mom began speaking with a woman in the VIP room, and although I was unimpressed with her name at the time, she was Cornelia Wallace, who had recently divorced from the notorious governor of Alabama, George Wallace. We seemed to meet famous people almost everywhere we went. My mom always handled herself with such poise and grace. *She really has this meeting people down,* I thought to myself. I always followed my mom's lead and credit her with my blossoming into a graceful girl throughout the poster child process.

As we returned home to Atlanta, we had only a couple of days before our next appearance at the Sheraton Hotel. This appearance was special, as it was the official announcement of me being the 1980 national poster child. It was September 25, 1979. As I stood on stage with my friend from a previous trip, Arnold Palmer, he announced my position. I looked out into the audience, and the love and support of my family, friends and neighbors were overwhelming. Just beyond, I could see my first-grade teacher, Ms. Bryant, in the audience as well. A wave of emotion rushed over me, and my eyes welled up with tears of joy and happiness. I could feel the energy of love in that room, and it was overwhelming. A look from Mr. Palmer gave me instant reassurance, and as he held me, we talked with each other before the microphone.

"I met this young lady a few weeks ago and knew the moment I met her she was someone special," he stated. "We have a commercial coming out soon, and her very own film will be released as well. The name of the film is *A Girl Named Betsy ...*" And with those words, the lights dimmed, and everyone's attention turned and focused on the movie screen in the front of the room.

As my movie played, I noticed there was not a dry eye in the room. I felt relieved as I had this wave of emotion come over me earlier and I no longer had to hold the tears back. It was an enlightening moment in my life where I knew my purpose was to help those in need and give others hope for the future.

The conference continued a while longer after the showing of the film. I spoke with various people from local and national television channels and radio stations. As I signed March of Dimes postcards and posters that were printed to commemorate the day, pictures and photos were being taken of me by the local newspapers.

"Betsy, we will need to start to tell everyone good-bye. We have to get you to Fort Worth for your next assignment," Nancy said as she knelt down beside me.

I would be flying to Fort Worth to meet the previous national poster child. She would officially give up her title to me, and I would continue the national poster child duties. It was a symbolic ceremony the March of Dimes had their poster children participate in, passing the crown down from one ruler to the next, except it was the national banner that was passed between the children.

I nodded to Nancy in agreement as I gave everyone a few last smiles and pleasant good-byes. She spoke with the reporters and photographers and gracefully let them know we were off to the airport. They wrapped up their work diligently with a few more photos as we were leaving.

As I sat in the car with my mom, Nancy, and the rest of my family, I was glad Dad was able to drive us to the airport. I knew it would be a few days before I saw him again and appreciated the time we had together.

As we entered the airport, we were met by several Delta attendants and more photographers. Dozens of pictures were taken at the check-in gate, and many of our friends showed up to see us off. I said my good-byes to my dad and siblings and shed a few tears with them as I hugged them good-bye. Mom and Nancy held my hands as we walked down the hallway to the plane. A flight attendant presented me with a bouquet of flowers and escorted us to the plane where we were seated in first class. My title of national poster child was announced on the airplane, and everyone clapped. I waved to the people on board and gave out postcards. The captain and a little boy on the flight both wanted to have their pictures taken with me, so Mom snapped away. It was another surreal moment where I realized I was here to give people hope.

When we arrived in Fort Worth, we were driven to the Marriott where we would be staying. On the marquee outside of the hotel were the words "Welcome Betsy Burch!" When we got to the hotel room, I immediately proclaimed it my favorite of all of them so far, entirely because it had a nightlight and a radio. Still, it was unimpressive compared to some of the rooms we would later stay in. I played and explored the room while Mom addressed some of the postcards that featured a picture of me in my roller skates on the front.

We went to eat that night with Melanie, who was the 1979 March of Dimes poster child, her parents, and Nancy. Melanie and I were very inquisitive with each other, and the restaurant announced us over the loudspeaker. The manager came over to our table to deliver our meals along with a huge cake and a sucker for each of us girls. Mine broke when I bit into it, and I started to get upset, but all was resolved when the manager brought a new one. One of the things I would have to learn in the following months was how to not be carried away and changed by the constant attention. Mom would prove instrumental in coaching me through this and reminding me that I was still Betsy, humble and blessed.

Mom seemed relieved to get back to the room after dinner. I think we had both felt a little intimidated by our previous-year's counterparts as they both seemed so well accustomed to their roles. Everything was new to Mom and me, and at the present moment, we had no way of knowing then that we too would grow more comfortable and confident in the coming year. It was in moments such as these that we leaned on each other and our bond grew even stronger. Through the strength of each other, we knew we would get the hang of this national publicity.

In the hotel room, we decided not to analyze any more of the evening and found simple pleasure in just being mom and daughter. As I got ready for bed, Mom was unwinding by reading a book. I sat on the edge of the bed and unbuckled the straps from around my waist and then the one on my thigh. This set my prosthesis free, and my leg always felt relieved to get some fresh air to it. I removed the socks that were on my short leg and laid them on top of the prosthesis on the floor. It was a ritual I performed every night and then again in reverse each morning. Even at my young age, I realized the blessings that had been bestowed upon me with the gift of being able to walk. My leg was just the means to do it, and for that I was grateful.

As the sun peeked through the hotel window, Mom and I performed another ritual, this time getting ready for our appearances that day. She helped me get my dress on and as always laid my socks on top of my shoes. I placed my socks and shoes on, and we went down to the hotel restaurant for a quick breakfast before meeting Nancy. The day consisted of visiting a series of newspapers for interviews and pictures, followed by a visit to the Fort Worth Children's Hospital. Here I was presented with a key to the city. It was among the first of what would turn out to be a long list of gifts that were given to me over the course of many months, and later we would make a lifetime of savoring the memories attached to those items.

As we toured the hospital, particularly the intensive care nursery, many pictures were taken. There were several done of me inside the nursery with the babies.

Afterward, we had lunch at the March of Dimes offices before returning to our hotel room. We were thankful for a bit of reprieve and rest from the day's events as we knew there were more assignments and appearances later that evening. We would be having dinner with the president of Southland Corporation— the company behind 7-11 stores. They were generous supporters of the March of Dimes.

Just as we were getting comfortable, there was a knock at the hotel door, and a gentleman informed us of a delivery from Southland Corporation.

"Ma'am, sorry to disturb you, but I have a special delivery for Betsy Burch," he informed my mom.

She nodded to confirm he had the correct room as she signed the receipt. *A delivery for me?* I thought with excitement. As we laid the beautifully wrapped box on the bed, we opened it with delicate enthusiasm. Inside the box lay a beautiful dress, light pastel pink with dainty lace details on the sleeves and hem. It was a dress made for a princess, and as I held it up to the mirror and twirled around in circles, I had not a care in the world.

"Betsy this is a very special gift, and we will need to thank them tonight when we see them," Mom said to me, reminding me to be grateful yet humble upon receiving gifts.

"I will thank them," I said as we began getting dressed for the event.

Mom helped me put my new dress on, and as she finished

getting dressed, I gazed in the mirror once more, admiring the dainty lace on my dress.

We met Nancy in the lobby, and a driver was waiting for us outside the front of the hotel. As I sat in the backseat, I could hear Mom and Nancy talking about the generous gift I had received earlier.

Nancy explained, "They are huge supporters of the March of Dimes and have been very generous with their donations. Jim is the gentleman we will be having dinner with tonight as well as a handful of other executives of the corporation."

I listened intently to Nancy and Mom discuss the events of the evening, as I knew it would benefit me to know some of the details. I had become familiar with the formalities of these dinner events, and I learned at the young age of six that it was with grace and poise that I should handle them. These experiences also provided me with wisdom and maturity.

As we arrived at the Reunion Tower at the Hyatt Regency, Jim greeted us with elation. There were photographers present, and many pictures were taken of me with executives of the corporation. The dinner appeared very strange to me, as courses were served one at a time. I started to grow taxed from the day's events and became frustrated with the procession of dinner. Nancy gently took my hand, and we walked outside.

"Betsy, you are doing a great job. I know you are tired, but if you can hang in there a bit longer, we will head back to the hotel."

"I just miss home and school," I said, tears slipping down my cheeks. "This restaurant is too fancy, and I don't understand why they keep serving us one thing at a time," I stated, as I had no idea what a five-course meal entailed.

As we sat outside the restaurant on a bench, Nancy did her best to explain the rubrics of these fancy dinners and the importance of me being there. She also reminded me I was a smart girl but noticed I was starting to use certain behaviors to get what I wanted.

"So, you'll have to be smart enough to stop it too, Betsy. You don't want to be that kind of poster child," she said with loving intention. As we sat there, she coached me on the importance of not utilizing this behavior and reminded me of the grace and poise I possessed. It was hard to swallow at this young age, as it prompted me to mature quite quickly. I sighed with reluctant acceptance.

As we went back inside, I felt somewhat renewed after my talk with Nancy, and the dinner finished uneventfully. As we were riding back to the hotel, I found comfort in the plush seats of the car and placed my head on Mom's shoulder, quickly falling asleep. When we got back to our room, Mom called home, as she knew I was missing my dad and siblings. We talked to Dad and Sara and John. Dad said there were some great write-ups in the papers about me. It gave me reassurance as I spoke with my siblings and dad. I still missed them but was able to get past the sad feelings of being away from home. I crawled into bed and fell asleep without hesitation.

The following morning, we met Melanie and her parents at their house. Melanie and I played tag, and I blossomed being around another child. Mom felt bad that I was missing out on being around other children my age over the course of the year but also knew she would take advantage of opportunities such as these in order for me to be around kids. We spent the day with them, and Mom found comfort in bonding with Melanie's mom, Ann. It was comforting to hear about their experiences from the previous year, as it provided Mom with helpful advice.

Ann was attractive and very well dressed—easily intimidating in both regards. It is easy to make ourselves feel less than we are when we start to compare ourselves with others. I think the fact that Mom understood this is why she was not only secure within herself but also so good with me, prompting me to always feel capable and strong. She would remind me that although others may appear one way, we do not know the burdens they carry.

She would remind me to have compassion not only for others but also for ourselves and to be grateful for our blessings.

The following days included interviews with TV stations and newspapers in Dallas, more appearances with Southland Corporation, and trips to City Hall. At City Hall, we met Mayor pro tem Bill Blackburn, who presented me with an honorary citizen plaque.

As our assignment in Dallas concluded, Nancy prepped me for my upcoming itinerary in Los Angeles, which we would embark on in the morning. As we said good-bye to Texas, I was excited about my trip to Los Angeles.

The following day upon boarding our American Airlines flight to California, I made the rounds on the airplane, met all of the flight attendants, talked with passengers, and handed out postcards. I was very much at home on planes by then. One of the stewardesses took a particular liking to me, and I to her, and she let me sit in her little fold-down seat at the front of the plane.

As the plane approached Los Angeles, I thought how huge the city looked from the air. Upon landing, my presumption proved correct. We stepped out onto the sidewalk, and I was overwhelmed with the number of cars everywhere. I also made a comment about the "smoke" in the air, referring to the prevalence of smog that surrounded me.

The Los Angeles events were rather unorganized, and we were expected to stay up late on our first night there, despite the fact that we'd been going nonstop for three days. We didn't have time to stop by the hotel after we got in but were whisked away to a bicycle shop for promotional photos for a March of Dimes bicycling fundraiser. From there we went to the actual event in an open-field arena, and I was introduced to the crowd. I stood up and waved to everyone, encouraged by the roar of their clapping.

By the time we arrived at the hotel, it was nearly midnight, and I had fallen asleep in the car. Mom told me the next morning that I'd slept through her unloading the luggage and carrying me to bed. We ended up in the twenty-first-floor penthouse, which she didn't even realize until she stepped off the elevator, and I didn't realize until the next morning when I woke up in a huge, oversized bed with many pillows.

That morning was the start of a day off for us, and Mom took me to Disneyland, another event she felt would help me in regards to having childlike activities in my life. It was a special day with Mom, and I enjoyed meeting all the Disney characters and having pictures made with them. As the day ended, we headed back to the hotel.

Upon returning to our room, Mom noticed that the gold cross necklace she had left on the dresser was all tangled up and that another necklace she'd left there was missing. It was a hurtful end to the day.

As we sat there together, the phone rang, and it was Sara. She just wanted to talk to Mom, and I think she cried on the phone. She was having a tough time with Mom being gone. That was the first time I really saw how hard it was for Mom to be away from home. She would tell me, years later, that she hadn't foreseen how difficult it would be to separate herself from life at home and how much time she would spend feeling that she'd caused a rift there. Still, Mom reminded me often through it all that family was something to be thankful for. Knowing what really mattered helped keep things in perspective.

The following days were occupied with a myriad of events and intervening lulls. This was how the remainder of our year of travels would go. A full day generally began with pictures with local government officials and proceeded to luncheons and focused promotional events. During our time off, we tried to see as many sites as we could and enjoy the local flavor of each new locale. In Los Angeles, we went to Beverly Hills and drove through Hollywood on a tour of the stars' homes. Mom loved that, but once again I didn't know who many of the people were.

The days also included many appearances with stars of the

time. This included meeting Magic Johnson and Johnny Carson, appearances on the *Dinah Shore Show*, and meeting Erik Estrada. As a child fan of the TV show *CHiPs*, my excitement took over me upon meeting him.

As I stood in the drive of MGM studios waiting for his arrival, I was filled with excitement and enthusiasm. The sound of a motorcycle was drawing near and then came into full view. *It's him!* I thought as I saw him getting close. He stepped off the motorcycle in the full uniform of his *CHiPs* character. His hair was dark as night and contrasted nicely with his tan skin. I was smiling ear to ear. He reached out to me, and I liked him immediately. As he knelt down, I sat on one of his knees. It was a moment I will never forget and which was thankfully captured by all the photographers around us.

Me and Erik Estrada, Los Angeles
Photo courtesy March of Dimes

"What's this?" he asked looking down at the cake I held in my hands. I'd brought him a cake with two frosted motorcycles on it.

"It's for you," I said, elated.

We had a multitude of pictures taken together outside and again inside the police station office that was part of the set. He was very personable and eager to help the March of Dimes. I will always have fond memories of this event and would brag about it the most over the years.

The day was winding down, and being tired from the events of the day, my mom and I welcomed the rest back in our hotel room. There was a message for Mom to call the night manager waiting for us. She assumed it had to do with the necklace incident the day before, as she had mentioned it to the manager.

"Yes, ma'am, if it's all right, may I just run up to the room now? It will only take a moment," the voice on the other end of the line stated.

"Yes. That will be fine," said Mom.

A few moments later, there was a knock at the door.

"I am so sorry to bother you this evening, but I wanted to deliver this in person as soon as I could," said the manager as he held out a small box for my mom.

As she opened the box, I caught a glimpse of the beautiful necklace inside, more expensive than the one stolen from the room. She was hesitant to take it and did not know what to say.

"I do hope you accept my sincerest apology for your necklace being stolen. I know this doesn't replace your other necklace, but I hope you will accept it on behalf of the hotel and staff," the manager said kindly.

"Yes, and I really appreciate the gesture. It means a lot to me. This wasn't necessary but thank you very much," Mom said.

He nodded and told Mom to let him know if he could do anything else while we were staying in the hotel. He and Mom exchanged a few more nice words, and as she closed the door, I could see the gratitude in her face.

The next morning, a package arrived from my teacher with a stack of assignments in it. Mom had made arrangements to coordinate with Mrs. Bryant and to teach me the first-grade curriculum herself while we were on the road. I was excited to receive the package and did my schoolwork for a while before it was time to get dressed for a banquet. Being an eager learner and yearning for school, I almost made my way through the entire stack of assignments on the first day. Mom had to remind me of the time in order to get dressed for the dinner banquet. She laid a dress on the bed for me, and I knew that was my cue to begin getting ready. I would always get my dress and lacey socks on and let Mom fuss over my hair. We had this routine down and were becoming very efficient at the task.

The banquet was held in the atrium at the hotel, around a huge fountain. I often got lost staring into the ripples in the water as the fountain splashed. The sound of the water was a good change compared to the bustling of the cocktail waiters and waitresses scurrying busily around the room. I did my best to meet and greet the people there, as they were supporters of the March of Dimes. There were also parents who had children with birth defects. Mom was an inspiration to these parents, and she always took the time to give them her undivided attention. She would talk with them and give them hope, and in return, these times were especially rewarding for Mom. She felt as if she made a difference in their lives, inspiring them to never give up. The night concluded, like many other banquets I attended, with a showing of the promos and film I had made earlier that year.

As our days in LA dwindled, we managed to have a day at the ocean before our final assignments in Los Angeles. Mom always enjoyed being near the water, as she grew up in Florida and spent many days on Daytona Beach. As we made our way down to the ocean, the water looked so enticing, with crystal clarity. I looked out upon the sea and saw the vastness and allure of the water, and marveled at how small and big I felt all at the same time.

The beach was at the bottom of a rocky bluff with a house perched on top of it like it may fall at any moment. My mom and I built castles in the sand. As the waves crashed in behind us, the power of the water was gentle and strong, complementing and contrasting. I felt normal for this moment, just me being with my mom on a beach, building castles in the sand. It was a good change from the previous days of endless appearances, interviews, and pictures. As I basked in the healing rays of the sun and the smell of the salty air coming off the ocean, I found peace and serenity in all that nature provided. Moments such as these gave me renewed hope and belief in myself, despite my physical differences. I would come to appreciate the beauty of the earth and nature more so later in life on my journey of spiritual enlightenment. Even then, I found the universe's treasures to be healing to both the emotional and spiritual realms of my being.

The last few days of our trip consisted of an endless round of luncheons and interviews and photographs, but the most notable thing about our time there was that we had such positive feedback from people. They complimented my mom and me and thanked us for what we were doing. We heard so many stories and saw such a gathering together of people who wanted to help children.

We knew our next assignment would begin the following day, so we turned in early on this night in order to get some rest. The next day, we said our good-byes to Los Angeles and boarded the plane for our next stop in Denver. As I gazed out of the airplane window from my seat, I saw the vastness of the Grand Canyon. My mind tried to comprehend the greatness of this work of nature. I imagined the stories behind it and the people that had been there before me. I drifted off into a light sleep, dreaming of the stories the canyon held. When I woke up, we were getting ready to land, and I was excited to see the sights of Denver.

From the airport, a representative from the local chapter, Marilyn, picked us up and drove us to our hotel. Along the drive, we saw rows and rows of aspen trees with their leaves turning orange. I admired their ever-flowing beauty and great stature. The wind on my face felt warm, and I again found comfort in the beauty of nature.

We jumped right into our assignment that evening by attending a banquet, and the following days were just as busy. The days were filled with meetings and photo shoots with various people. This included meeting the mayor and interviewing with local radio stations. Denver was proving to be another very busy assignment, and I seemed to fall into the differentiating roles with natural ability, whether at fancy gala dinners or simple photo shoots with various people and corporations. In a short time, I had made quite the transition from being local poster child to that of a national one.

The weather changed quickly, and it was bitterly cold the following day. That night we were off for yet another dinner, this time at the Chateau Pyrenees, which was elegant and spacious with a huge grand piano at the center. All the girls were given carnations to wear and a book of matches with our name on it. I felt quite grown up to be included in this. Whenever the ladies pulled out a cigarette, there was always a gentleman or a waiter coming forward with a light. The table glittered with cocktails in crystal glasses and elegantly displayed food courses.

Over the events of the following days it rained and snowed. We met the governor, posed for more pictures, ate, shopped, and swam in the pool. The days were beginning to all look the same, and just about then it was time to leave again. Mom packed up our things while I tried to help, but really there wasn't much to do because it wasn't looking like it was all going to fit. Finally, Mom got everything zipped in, and even though our suitcases were bulging, I was happy we wouldn't be leaving anything behind.

The next day found us up in the air again. We changed planes in St. Louis and met with another March of Dimes poster child at the airport. It being October, she gave us a pumpkin, and the two of us posed for at least a dozen photos.

We landed in Louisville, Kentucky, and were taken to the Marriott. Up we went to our room, and I let out a little squeal when the doors opened. Mom told the folks at home later that she nearly fainted. We had the Kentucky Derby Suite, a huge room with a king-sized bed, TV and console, dining area, couch, and dresser. In the bathroom, there was a refrigerator beside an enormous tub. Adjoining this was another bedroom with two beds, which I immediately claimed as my own room. On the large table in the center of the main room were a dozen roses in a vase and a stack of letters for us.

Our schedule was pretty light in Kentucky and consisted of two banquets and some photo shoots. The banquets for me had become quite routine, as they followed the same format, which consisted of mingling, followed by fancy dinner courses, introductions, and then closing with my film and promo shoots and dancing.

Back in the room, we talked on the phone to everyone at home. Mom was happy that Sara and John were both doing well, and Dad said he missed us both very much. When it came time for bed, the room of my own suddenly didn't seem so exciting, and I ended up crawling into the huge king bed with Mom.

The next morning, we had grits for breakfast. It was the first place so far on the road that had grits on the menu, and we both dug in. We passed the day in the same fashion as the rest, by swimming, playing, doing schoolwork, and eating. I loved the restaurant we went to that day because they served me a banana split almost as big as I was. I was also getting excited that Dad would be joining us on the next leg of our journey—to Washington, DC.

We finished our assignment in Kentucky and, over the weekend, flew to Washington, DC, in preparation for our next task. On Monday morning, we went to the Pentagon escorted by two members of the air force. There we met General Lew Allen Jr., the chief of staff, and he presented me with an air force pin, a record, and a framed photograph. We posed together while the cameras snapped away and then went on a long trek down the hallways, which in total were seventeen miles, they told us. But we only had to go so far as the assistant joint chief of staff, General Postay's, office. We were then escorted into a reception room and were formally introduced to General Postay, who in turn told the twenty-five or so people present about me and presented me with a beautiful engraved medal.

"We figured you'd love this gift, Betsy, because we knew a little girl would probably prefer it to a cake made up just for her," he joked.

My eyes got big when I saw the cake; it was huge with a clown face painted onto it in frosting. Admiral Hayward of the navy pinned a navy stickpin to my shirt. And when all the festivities were done and it was time to go, we retraced our path down the long hallway. While we were proceeding toward the exit, a guard stopped us and asked what I was carrying.

I showed him the picture.

"Miss," he said, "you'll need a property pass to carry that out of here."

And he was dead serious. So he and Mom tended to the paperwork, and I looked around in wonder at the official looking place with its rows of office doors lining the corridor in both directions. At the end of the hall, a door opened, and an elderly gentleman stepped out to confer with another officer.

Our escort leaned down and said to me, "That there is General Bradley. He's ninety-six years old and a five-star general."

I didn't know exactly what that meant, but I was pretty impressed.

Nancy overheard this and began working her magic, trying to earn us an opportunity to meet the five-star general. She disappeared for a moment, and upon return, she knelt down to me.

"Betsy, we are heading down this hallway to meet General Bradley," she said.

I agreed, as I'd learned impromptu meetings could happen in this role.

As I approached General Bradley's office, I could see the seriousness in those around me. Although I was unaware of the importance of this man, those around me knew it, and I followed their lead. As we entered the room, I saw a very elderly gentleman sitting down behind a desk. I was gently prompted by Nancy to walk over to him. He smiled with great acceptance of me and acknowledged my physical differences in a blink of his eye. He motioned me closer, and I stood next to him and smiled back with mutual admiration; there was nothing less than respect and admiration in the age span between us of ninety years. We saluted each other and knew we had both overcome many struggles; some included fights on the battlefield, while others included fighting to stay alive in this life to make

a difference. It was an awe-inspiring moment for us both. It was a moment that changed both of our lives, for the better.

It had been a very long and tiring day so far, but I was counting down the hours until my dad arrived. Finally, it was time to meet him at the airport, and it felt strange

Me and General Omar Bradley, the only five-star general at the time
Photo courtesy March of Dimes

to be there picking someone else up for a change. When I saw Dad walking toward me in the long airport corridor, I picked up my pace, and we met somewhere in the middle. I was so glad to see him. I immediately began telling him of the events of the day and informed him of the people we met. He seemed impressed about us meeting General Bradley. I was just happy to have him with us on the remainder of my assignment there. We were given the night off from events, and we spent it as a family having dinner and then getting a good night's sleep.

The next day was a whirlwind of meetings and photographs.

We went to the Capitol building, where we waited in the Senate receiving offices, and two pages began bringing the senators in to meet me one at a time. With each, I posed for two photographs and got a signed autograph. We had lunch in the Senate dining room, and Senator Warner and Senator Goldwater took me onto the Senate floor. The rest of the day consisted of more photos and more meetings with congressmen. We met with forty-nine in all, including Senator Kennedy. I gave him a rose, and we talked a little bit. When he turned to leave, I said, "Aren't you going to give me a kiss since I gave you a rose?"

All of the adults in the room were dumbfounded, including him, but they all began to chuckle, and he came back with a big smile and kissed me on the cheek.

As the day turned into evening, we had dinner, and I knew Dad was leaving in the morning. He travelled quite frequently with his job and only had a day he could spend with us in Washington before heading back home to care for my siblings. I was a bit sad that evening but tried to enjoy what time I had left to visit with him. The next morning came too fast, and it was time to drop Dad off at the airport.

When he was gone and Mom and I turned to leave, I broke down. "I don't want him to go," I cried.

"I know, Betsy. I don't either."

I could tell that Mom was upset too. This was another moment when the bond between my mom and I would only grow stronger. It was just the two of us again, and we found comfort in knowing we had each other. We went back to the hotel room, and she ordered up some cheesecake to make us feel better. The guy who delivered it to us was very sweet and brought up a flower for each of us. It was the little things and the small kindnesses of the people we met that made the experience so much richer.

From our country's capital, we were off to Virginia to make an appearance at the Redskins training camp where we met with the players and coach. The Redskins were big supporters of the March of Dimes. I took several pictures with Coach Pardee and the team. The players were very nice and compassionate. I ended up with a signed football, T-shirt, and loads of pennants and decals. We watched them practice for a while before we had to get to the airport, as we were getting ready to fly home. I was ready to go home for a few days. This had been the longest stretch of being away from my family, friends, and school to date. It was a tradeoff of course, missing my home in exchange for the experience of a lifetime.

As we were settling into our life and daily routine in Stone Mountain, I enjoyed the normalcies of home and school. Back at school, everything went great, and the kids were as excited to see me as I was to see them. Mrs. Bryant was lovely and called my mom with a good report after my first day back. October was closing out, and the cool fall weather was here to stay. I felt as if the month of October was flying by, but I was more than fine with that as I was excited for Halloween. I was just like any other six-year-old on Halloween night; I loved going trick-or-treating in my costume.

On Halloween night, my siblings and I walked around our neighborhood until there wasn't a single house we hadn't visited. We had three bags stuffed with candy. It was a great way to send off our visit home, for the next morning we were scheduled to leave again, this time for Memphis, Tennessee.

For Mom, time passed a little more slowly. She was caught up in doing countless household chores to get everything running smoothly before we were to leave again. There was a flurry of family visits. Gran left, and my Dad's mom came to stay at the end of the month, in preparation for us leaving again.

Dad drove us to the airport when it was time to go. I picked up on the solemn moods of my parents. All the travelling appeared to have taken quite a toll on my family. It was an uneasy moment in the car as I tried not to feel like it was my fault for the tension. I would learn later in life, there were many solemn moments such as these between my parents, but it took me becoming older to understand the impact it would one day have.

As we arrived at the airport, Mom and Dad said their good-byes, and I hugged my dad good-bye. My mom and I made our way into the airport, something we had become quite accustomed to. Our next stop was Memphis, Tennessee, where we were scheduled to visit Elvis Presley's home at Graceland.

Our flight was uneventful, and after settling into our room at the Hyatt Regency, we dressed for the photo shoot in Graceland. My mom was excited about this but saddened too to see where Elvis was buried and to remember his tragic story. The grounds were beautiful but seemed to be just sitting there, languishing, after all that they had once been. Our trip in Memphis continued with a series of luncheons and mass photo shoots. Mom and I both spoke at the luncheons and banquets as we always did and had become quite comfortable in our roles at these events. It was a time to share our story and hopefully inspire others along the way.

Our time in Memphis was coming to a close, and our next stop would be Indiana to do a promotional shoot with Kenny Rogers at his concert. I was very aware of who Kenny Rogers was, and I was more than excited to have my next assignment with him. He was a huge supporter of the March of Dimes.

Our visits weren't always made of roses and fancy dinners, though. We never knew from one city to the next what awaited us. The hotel in Tennessee was crawling with mold, and Nancy had roaches in hers. She called the front desk, and the manager came to inspect the rooms. There was nothing he could do but agree that the conditions were deplorable, and we packed up our bags, and Nancy had to scramble to book rooms elsewhere. These little glitches ended up mostly being inconvenient but sometimes bordered on being downright awkward.

Mom and I had our tiffs about homework as well. We were never on a set schedule, so she had to make time for my studies whenever she could. Of course this didn't always sit well with me when I wanted to be doing something else. She rarely lost her temper, but when she did, I knew it was time to buckle down and get to work. The day we went to see Kenny Rogers was one of those days. I imagine the experience of that year was much different for Mom than for me, due to our differing levels of responsibility and our different perspectives.

We managed to complete all of my school assignments, and we were looking forward to a fun night with Kenny Rogers. We walked into the theater in the middle of Dottie West singing in her smoky voice and sat in the third row, just in front of the stage through most of the Oakridge Boys' set. Then Nancy pulled us backstage. We met Kenny's crew, and just before it was time for him to go on stage, Kenny Rogers came out of his dressing room in a purple suit. I ran up to him as if I'd known him all my life.

"Hi, Betsy," he said, and bent down to shake my hand. "Hey, you're missing a tooth! Did you know that?"

I nodded and laughed. Taking his hand, we went to sit down. Pictures were taken, and he signed autographs for me and Mom and everyone at home.

"Do you want to sing a little bit with me?" he asked.

"Yes!" I replied.

"Well then, let's see. What song do you want to sing?"

We ended up singing a little bit of "Lucille," and he told me I did great.

He continued with me sitting on his lap, and as he sang to me and played his guitar, what felt like millions of photographs were taken. It was another one of those moments you never forget, even at the

Me and Kenny Rogers
Photo courtesy March of Dimes

young age of six. His time on the concert stage was approaching, and a few last hugs and smiles were exchanged.

My mom, Nancy, and I were seated in the front row for the remainder of the concert. I couldn't help but think he was singing directly to me as he looked out into the front row.

The next morning, as we were checking out of the hotel, we saw that Kenny and I had made the front page of the Evansville newspaper, so we grabbed a copy on our way out of town. I was thrilled.

From Indiana, we went to Chicago, where it was quite a whirlwind. We were greeted with bouquets and corsages and picked up in a blue limousine driven by a chauffeur in a sleek black suit.

Our first stop was McDonald's where we met Ronald McDonald himself. I also met the local poster child, and she presented me with a Chicago T-shirt and a tote bag for my mom. Afterward, we were driven to the Schubert Theater where we watched *Annie*.

We stayed at the Drake Hotel in Chicago, which was a very old hotel. Our room was vast with a multitude of adjoining doors. In the days that we were there, we met a multitude of sponsors and had dinners with various people. One particular night, we had dinner with the actress who played Annie, Mary Lombardi. I had a wonderful evening with her and cried when it was time to go. I loved meeting so many people, but I often missed being around kids and felt it keenly whenever I had an opportunity to interact with another child.

After Chicago, we stopped in Atlanta for a day, and when we arrived at the airport, we were greeted by a whole entourage, including Dad, Sara, John, two Six Flags characters, Atlanta Braves mascot Chief Noc-A-Homa, and Atlanta weatherman Guy Sharpe. As our tour progressed, we could feel the momentum picking up, and not only did more people recognize me, but more people received us and wanted to take part in what we were doing with March of Dimes. Our family got to stay together in a hotel that night and attend a banquet, which was the usual fare but different and nice because we were all together.

From there, Mom and I were on our own again, headed for Norfolk, Virginia. Here we went to the Naval Air Station and went aboard several of the Navy ships. Aboard the USS *Beary*, we had refreshments, and I got to steer the ship. We were served lunch and given a tour by the sailors on the USS *Emory Land*. My favorite by far were the helicopters they let me sit in because the nice captain who showed me around told me that they were just like the one the president rode in.

Boston was our next stop, and we were met there by a large group of March of Dimes folks and three local poster children. Mom was particularly taken with the little boy, Raymond, who was living then with a foster mother. Among our Boston stops were the Pepsi Cola factory where we were laden with gifts, and the Celtics stadium where I had my picture taken with several players and watched a game.

After Boston came Minnesota, where we stayed in a hotel right on the Mississippi River. From our room we could see the barges going by on the water. And I wasn't too excited about what happened there because I had my eyes set on our next trip ... back home for Thanksgiving!

15

The Source of Strength

Now, with the race under way, I felt good and strong. I'd worked hard to be where I was, and I was determined to not give up. I focused on putting one leg in front of the other and working my way upward, but then I looked around me and saw that I was only halfway up the incline of the bridge. I still had half of the climb ahead of me, and for the first time that day, I felt my spirit falter. What was I doing? My steps slowed, and I looked around for Eric, who turned and smiled from just ahead of me. I drew my strength from him, just as I'd drawn it from my mother and from my experiences as a child. I had overcome so much and believed that I could do this too. But I would be lying if I said I never had a doubt.

16
An End and a Beginning

The great thing about being in the public eye for the March of Dimes was that we met a lot of great people who had their own stories about friends or loved ones with birth defects or other debilitating issues. It was so easy to connect to strangers when we were united by a common bond and an achievable goal, which was what the March of Dimes gave to us.

On the plane back home from one of our cross-country jaunts, we met a woman who'd had polio as a child. Back then, the March of Dimes had still been serving the vision of Franklin D. Roosevelt in fighting polio. This woman teared up as she told us that the March of Dimes had bought her shoes for twelve years.

Later, my mom said, "That was no coincidence, Betsy. There were so many empty seats in the plane, but we ended up next to her."

It gave more validation to what we were doing to know it had an effect on people's lives and that there was a greater mission at stake.

We spent Thanksgiving in Florida with Gran, my mom's mom. Thanksgiving was always a special time for me as a child because I loved going to my grandmother's house. Gran and I were extremely close, and I treasured every moment I spent with her. She cooked Thanksgiving dinner each year, and she had a natural hand for cooking; no one left the table hungry. It was one of the rare times when our family could be together without the worry of the next deadline for the March of Dimes.

My mom and I were off for a few days from our travels and assignments and enjoyed the much-needed break. We stayed up late watching television after finishing our Thanksgiving meal, and it was the simplest of days. There was no such thing as cable back then but rather a tuning antenna. A knob on top of the TV could be turned to try to improve reception, and we kids would take turns fiddling with it. There was so much beauty in the simplicity of days like those.

Gran lived in the country in Ocala, Florida, where Spanish moss hung from the oak trees and arrowheads could still be found on walks through her property. Indians once lived where she did, and their spirit was always with us in the background. Across the street from her house, there remained a circular imprint in the ground where the Indians once danced. I was fascinated by this as a child and had many stories in my head on what life was like back when the Indians lived there. *If only the trees could talk,* I thought to myself.

Moments with Gran always went by too fast, and as soon as we got back to Atlanta after Thanksgiving, Nancy called and told us our next assignment would be a meeting with President Carter. On this particular assignment, the whole family was invited. It had not been long since we were in Washington, DC, on our previous assignment; however, I felt this one was a bit more official since we were meeting the president.

The following week found us arriving in our nation's capital. We were all excited about the privilege and experience of meeting the president. We arrived a day prior to our meeting at the White House. The evening was spent as a family over dinner, during which time we all pondered what the next day might hold.

When the day itself arrived, we all dressed in our nicest out-fits and headed for the White House. I was dressed in a red velvet dress with the March of Dimes banner pinned from my shoulder to my waist. On the way there, I was full of questions, and my parents did a good job of explaining, despite my mom being a little nervous. Security checked my parents' driver's licenses at the gate and then opened it for us to drive through. We parked outside the West Wing, and the guards there took our names. Several people came out to greet us and direct us into the house and through the hall-ways. They took us to the Cabinet room, and there were sev-eral chairs there. The tallest belonged to the president, and I thought maybe he was a very tall man.

Me and President Carter, Oval Office
Photo courtesy March of Dimes

The room was full of members of the press, and we didn't see him at first for the crowd and the flashing of cameras, but then there he was in front of me, kneeling down so he could look me in the eye and shake my hand.

"They didn't tell me you were so pretty, Betsy," he said.

When he stood, he put his hand on my back to led us to his desk.

"Come on over," he told the rest of my family, and continued to ask me questions about myself while we walked before the press. My whole family gathered there, and introductions were made. The cameras kept flashing, especially as President Carter put his hands on my shoulders and introduced me before the TV reporters who were televising the event.

"Betsy is not only a beautiful young girl but a brave leader for an important cause."

He seemed a kind and gentle man. He signed a proclamation for the March of Dimes and an autograph for me, handing me the pen afterward. It was really an astounding experience, and I'll always consider moments like those foundational to my life. Being out there in front of people and being told that

Me and President Carter, Oval Office
Photo courtesy March of Dimes

what I was doing was good and brave made me feel unafraid of who I was. My parents had always told me that I could be and do anything, but these experiences really showed me that I could do so fearlessly.

When we got home, it was fun to hear how many people had seen us on TV with the president. More gifts awaited us at home, as well as stacks of letters from people we had met all over the country.

Two days later, Mom and I were off again, this time to Louisville, Kentucky, to meet with Colonel Sanders and the Kentucky Fried Chicken people again. It was the middle of December and a quick trip. Soon we would be heading back home again for the holidays.

Nancy called us as soon as we returned to Atlanta and asked how everything had gone. She also told us the details of the next leg of our tour. We would be filming a one-minute ad spot for the Sugar Bowl and appearing on *Good Morning America* for an interview with David Hartman. On New Year's Eve, we were due to head for New Orleans.

All of the brief stays at home were just enough to give us a break and get us excited to go back out on tour. I couldn't comprehend at that time how difficult some of our travel was on my mom. There were a whole host of complications for her, aside from the fact that she had to forfeit so much time with her two other children for over a year. It put a strain on her relationship with my father. As an adult, she also had to navigate the social intricacies of life on the road and meeting new people. It was an isolated time for her in many ways. Neither of us had been prepared for what the series of tours would demand of us. And when it was over, we would be thrust back into our old lives, expected to pick up exactly where we'd left off. For both of us, it would be bittersweet when that time came.

For now, the flights were quickly becoming one of my favorite parts of travelling. Many times the flight attendants would pamper me, and with that came perks of seeing behind-the-scenes workings of so many planes. We'd had a nice holiday at home and found ourselves in New Orleans on New Year's Eve. I slept through the whole New Year's celebration, and Mom tried to sleep beside me in spite of the revelry in the hall and adjoining rooms. The following day, we woke as the sun rose, and a whole new year stretched before us: 1980! It was the dawn of a new decade.

Game day was upon us, and on that day the Alabama Crimson Tide beat the Arkansas Razorbacks. We were at the game until halftime, both in a press box and out on the field at times. We had sideline seats. Two cheerleaders carried me around on their shoulders before the game, taking me around the entire dome while I waved and had a great time interacting with the fans.

Before the game began, I met the musician Pete Fountain, and he carried me to the end zone where I was introduced to the audience and a plug was given for the March of Dimes Mothers' March. A great round of applause followed, and it was exhilarating. Pete played a clarinet that he'd borrowed from a girl in the Alabama marching band and asked me if I wanted to play as well. I shook my head, only refusing because he'd had it in his mouth. Being so germ conscious was perhaps an indicator of my future plans to be a nurse.

We were driven to and from the game in a 1938 Hard Times Cadillac. It was a fun experience. There was a reception after the game in the hotel, and then we rode a horse-drawn carriage through the French Quarter. For me, these times were less exciting than those when I was in front of crowds of people and getting special attention, but it was no less magical to be in a new place surrounded by new sights, sounds, and smells. It was an experience I wish I had been old enough to enjoy and remember more.

January was a busy month, with multiple assignments, which meant many plane itineraries. On one particular plane trip to New York, I met a gentleman who was very intriguing to me. He was wearing a big, fluffy, hooded coat, and he had a beard. I appreciated the interesting aura he gave off, and I was glad to be sitting next to him on the plane.

With childlike innocence and lacking some general etiquette, I turned to him and said, "You look like an Eskimo."

He smiled and laughed, pulling his hood back.

"I'm not an Eskimo," he said kindly. "I'm Irish."

Nancy leaned over and asked him about his origins. "I'm Norwegian," she said, furthering the conversation.

"And what are you, Betsy?" he asked after we'd made our introductions.

"I'm the national poster child."

And really, that is how seriously I took the title. I had grown very comfortable in this role, and it showed when I talked about it to strangers.

After arriving in New York, we were taken to the Warwick Hotel downtown. It was winter in New York, and as the snowflakes were falling lightly outside, Mom and I walked down to Rockefeller Center and watched the ice skating. The white of the snowflakes around us contrasted nicely with the ice on the rink. People were skating, and they looked as if they were floating aimlessly and endlessly with no worries at all. I watched the skaters between the snowflakes; I took in the beauty of my surroundings. As each snowflake fell, I noticed the subtle differences in their shape and size. Just as we are all different, it's those very differences that make us beautiful. In my physical differences alone, I hoped there was some beauty to be found. We stood there for a while before eating lunch at the promenade above the rink.

On our way back to the hotel, we stopped by Radio City Music Hall to pose for photos with the Rockettes right before show time. They invited us to stay for the live Christmas program.

Me and the Rockettes, New York
Photo courtesy March of Dimes

While in New York, we also visited the UN ambassador's lodgings for a meet and greet accompanied by the usual bombardment of photos. This was followed by a trip to the Elizabeth Arden cosmetics offices where we met with the president of the company. When we left, they gave us a shopping bag full of their products, which delighted my mom. I was more interested of course in the little toys and trinkets that people seemed to offer me everywhere we went.

Back in the hotel, the sounds of the city never stopped, but I had no trouble sleeping. It was a bit more difficult for Mom—tomorrow was the big day. Mom was nervous as could be and spent the night before and the next morning preparing our clothes and getting us ready for my big, national television appearance on *Good Morning America*. But nothing could have prepared her for what actually took place on the following day.

Mom had already arranged for room service to bring me cereal, milk, and juice for breakfast. She rolled my hair while I ate, although I really just wanted to sleep some more. It was barely even light outside. But we were dressed, fed, and ready to go when the ABC network limousine pulled up to the front of the hotel at 7:45. We were greeted at the studio and taken to the green room where guests of the show waited to go on. Mom had coffee, and I talked with Nancy.

Eventually, one of the staffers came in and told us that Mom would not be going on air with me. A moment later, David Hartman came into the room, and I remembered him from the last time we'd met. He was nice and made me feel very special for being there.

Our time slot was scheduled for 8:39. Then, ten minutes before I was due to go on, one of the staff came in with a clipboard, looking frenzied.

"I'm afraid you've been bumped," she said. "We just acquired live satellite coverage of a man returning from Iran. The footage is going in your slot."

There was a collective sigh of disappointment from Mom and Nancy.

"Does this mean I can't be on the show?" I asked.

"It doesn't look like it."

I was disappointed as well. I liked filming TV spots. The March of Dimes had sent out memos to every chapter in the United States, and we had told everyone we knew to be watching TV this morning for my appearance. Well, it wasn't a total waste as I got to go into the studio after the live portion of the show and tape several spots. When I walked in, David called out, "Hellooo, Betsy!"

"Hellooo, David!" I called back.

One of the spots was a five-minute interview, and one was a bit piece in which I said, "Hello, I'm Betsy Burch from Stone Mountain, Georgia. Good morning, America!"

We had no idea if these would ever be aired, and Mom and Nancy were particularly depressed by how things had turned out, but I was happy with the fact that I'd gotten to sit in the studio while the cameras rolled and talk to David Hartman, a man I considered a friend. Plus, he gave me a big poster and signed it.

The limousine took us to the CBS studios next where we got to sit on the set and watch Eileen Fulton, who played Lisa on the soap opera *As the World Turns*. With the day nearly at an end, we walked back to the hotel. It was bitterly cold outside, and I was wearing a dress. They always had me wear dresses for TV appearances because it showed my prosthetic leg, and that was the image March of Dimes wanted to portray. The walking was getting uncomfortable because I was quickly growing out of my prosthesis. Mom noticed my limp. I usually never complained about my leg hurting, but Mom could read the discomfort on my face.

"Good thing we're going home," she said. "We'll have to make a trip to the doctor to get you fit with a new prosthesis."

"Yes, I do need an adjustment," I said as I held her hand a little tighter and we continued down the cold, crowded streets of the city.

As she said this, I once again accepted my fate of a lifetime of doctors' appointments and prosthetic fittings. It would always bring me down a little, but I tried to find the good in all things. And at this particular moment, I was thankful I was able to walk down the street beside my mom.

My real leg was red from the cold. It was twenty-nine degrees and dropping. The snow continued to fall in the big city, and I looked forward to the warmth of the hotel room.

We flew out of LaGuardia the following day, just before a big storm hit New York. We were homebound again. The whole year was full of these fits and starts. We were barely at home long enough to get any enjoyment out of it before we had to set off again. During that particular weekend visit home, our time was dominated by getting me fitted for a new prosthetic leg. After adjustments were made on my prosthesis, we were off on our next assignment in Texas.

Me and David Hartman
Photo courtesy March of Dimes

Our trip to Texas was in a bit of a shambles. Even though our representatives at the March of Dimes worked hard at coordinating everything, there were times when travels were very erratic and off schedule. This trip was one of those times. It was obviously not anyone's fault when our flights were delayed, and we found ourselves running through the airport on more than one occasion. When we arrived in Houston there was no one there to meet us, and we had to wait a long time before a man approached us and said, "Would you happen to have seen a poster child running around these parts?"

My mom looked at him with a confused expression. *Is this guy joking or does he really not know it is us?*

"Yes, it's us, sir," Mom politely stated, but she was weary from the less than smooth plane ride.

"Ma'am, I apologize for being late. The traffic here to the airport held me up." He smiled, as if in an attempt to ease the awkwardness.

"No problem. If you could get us to our hotel, we would appreciate it. It's been a long travel day," Mom said.

Without hesitation, the man helped us with our bags and showed us to the car. It was a relief to Mom and me to be in the right place, and we looked forward to getting some rest at the hotel.

When we arrived in our hotel in Houston, Mom received a call from the March of Dimes that my previous taped interview would be airing on the following morning's episode of *Good Morning America*. Mom called everyone she knew in the short amount of time available, including my school so the class could watch it, and also so Sara and John could be excused to watch it too.

The following morning, Mom and I watched the show on the TV in our hotel room. When David Hartman came on air to talk about me and the March of Dimes, he really made it sound like a big deal, and that made me feel good. Mom was beaming and couldn't have been happier with how it went. She was happy that my spot finally got to air.

In the following days, we drove all over Texas, it seemed, visiting small towns, shaking hands with mayors and touring oil refineries. The events were quite stuffy and time-consuming. There were associates with various oil companies to meet with, and we were growing weary of the airs we had to put on. We were ready to be finished with our assignment in Texas and looked forward to our next assignment in Alabama. On our departure day from

Texas, we gratefully boarded the plane to Alabama, and Mom quickly found her way to the bottom of two whiskey sours.

Alabama, however, wasn't much better than Texas. Mom and I were both tired from so much travel and airline debacles. In our down time, she tried to get me to do my schoolwork, but I whined a fair bit. Maybe it was our waning energy that allowed things to get under our skin, but everything that could go wrong seemed to. In Alabama, we continued to meet with various corporations that supported the March of Dimes.

From Montgomery, we caught a flight to Jackson, Mississippi. We sat in first class and were hopeful that this was a sign our trip would take a turn for the better. Our time in Mississippi was spent entirely on publicity. We filmed a live TV spot and a few interviews, attended a press conference, and recorded a few radio shows. On multiple occasions, I was taken out to dinner on my own or with other children affiliated with the March of Dimes. This meant that Mom had a few much-needed hours on her own.

From here we were off to Tulsa to take part in the March of Dimes Telerama telethon to raise money for the cause. This was one of my favorite events ever. On our way to the Camelot Inn, Mom gasped when she saw a billboard of me on the side of the highway. I was amazed at how huge it was.

The Telerama began that night, and we met Ted Lange who played Isaac on *The Love Boat*. But for me the great thing about the telethon was that there were bands, clowns, singing, dancing, and a general atmosphere of noisy entertainment. This went on for two days, and I got to sing a few songs of my own choosing and answered the phones during filming to say, "March of Dimes Telerama, this is Betsy." When it was all said and done, I had formed a pretty clear idea that telethons were what I wanted to be doing. Even Mom agreed that it was better than the publicity days. But there were still many more publicity events awaiting us.

The following day, we were off to Cleveland to meet the

mayor. A limousine drove us to his offices, and when I was getting out of the car, I hit a switch and locked all of the car doors with the car still running and the keys in the ignition. We had planned on bringing a box of fresh Georgia peaches to the mayor, but those were locked in the trunk too. Minor setback.

It turned out I was the first national poster child to visit Cleveland in fifteen years, and they gave us the warmest welcome imaginable. They wheeled out a great big birthday cake with my name on it and sang to me. It was worth every moment of what it took to get there, and Mom said I really came through even though we were tired and didn't get out of the reception until after midnight.

The rest of our time in Cleveland was spent on publicity spots, and then we were on to Wisconsin for more of the same. I participated in several promotional events and enjoyed being presented with more gifts and cakes for my upcoming birthday.

It was in Milwaukee that I got to meet Howie, who worked with the March of Dimes there. He was a kind man, and I was particularly taken with him. Mom told me much later that Howie made very little money doing what he did but loved the cause he worked for and the people he worked with. It was easy to tell that he had a big heart, and it was people like him who stood out to me and helped build the strength that I would carry with me for the rest of my life.

Once Wisconsin's events were concluded, we headed home for a very short reprieve of only four days. In this short time, my mom and I appreciated the time we had with the rest of our family. We managed to fit in a seventh birthday party for me, and Mom was busy, running around shopping and organizing the household.

Dad showed us the latest scrapbook he'd been working on of me while we were on assignment. It was his way of participating by organizing scrapbooks and souvenirs while Mom and I were away. These things I would come to cherish later in life as a chronicle of the events of my poster-child years.

In the following days, we were busy with appointments at the prosthetist's office again. The last time I was home, adjustments were made to get me through until I was home again. This visit, however, entailed more than adjustments. I was getting fitted for a new prosthesis altogether.

The process of acquiring a new prosthesis was quite involved back then. Many plaster molds were made of my short leg. After the molds were done, the prosthetist would begin the monotonous job of making a fitting from the mold. It would then require many fittings to iron out any rough edges, and for me, there were always many rough edges. Then came the hard steps of getting the alignment correct. The whole thing was draining for me emotionally, and I would oftentimes go into a slight depression and denial phase. New legs always felt very different from my previous prosthesis. My body was changing as I grew. Slipping into a consistent limp as I grew out of one prosthesis after another didn't help.

The continual waxing and waning of denial and depression took me back to those first feelings from when I had my amputation. I remembered Dr. King and my mom in my hospital room trying to get me up on crutches and the pain I felt. The physical pain of the amputation and the emotional pain of the loss of a limb was much to handle, even for a resilient child. Although I still had my right knee and about ten inches of leg below the knee, it was still a loss that required grieving. This grieving resurfaced each time a new prosthesis was made for me.

After a while of propping each new prosthesis in a corner, I would eventually succumb to acceptance and reluctantly put it on in lieu of the old one. After a while, the new prosthesis felt better and better, and I began living life again.

Before I knew it, we were off again, to Phoenix this time. On our last day home before leaving, we drove to Atlanta to pick up my new leg on the way to the airport. It was tough for the doctors to coordinate getting it ready between our travels, but they managed it well, and I was soon walking comfortably again.

On the flight to Phoenix, the flight attendants announced me over the intercom and told everyone I'd just turned seven years old. I was quite proud and felt grown-up as they asked me to help them serve the inflight meal and drinks. I spoke with almost everyone on the plane during this process and even collected a few donations for March of Dimes. Meanwhile, we passed over desert, mountains, snow, and the Rio Grande. Mom was having a harder time leaving home than usual, and she was quiet as we flew.

"Are you doing okay with this?" I asked her when I sat back down again, echoing a question she had asked me in the past and feeling very mature.

She smiled. "Of course I am. I'm very excited for whatever comes next."

Even though sincere, I could sense the hesitation in her voice. I knew Mom was growing weary of travelling and being away from home. I did my best to console her in the only way I knew how as a seven-year-old, by holding her hand.

The success of each trip depended a lot on the local chapter that was running our events. Some were better organized than others. Phoenix was one of those places where everything seemed a bit disorganized. We took a private plane to Yuma, and Mom and I watched ourselves on the news from our hotel room. We were there for a few television spots and then boarded another private plane, this time to Utah. To my delight, we were bound for Salt Lake City for another telethon.

On our first night there, we went to a cocktail party in the McCune Mansion in Salt Lake City. Everything was blue velvet and satin and marble. There was a red pool table and red velvet seats that looked like thrones, but my favorite item in the house was an elegant player piano. A piano that played itself—I'd never seen anything like it and was half-convinced it was magic.

The next day when we stepped out of the hotel, it was into a whole new world covered in white. It had snowed about four inches, and I played in it for the rest of the day.

From twelve degree temperatures in Utah, we headed for sunny San Diego. However, it was not so sunny that January. It was raining, and the flight was particularly bumpy and stressful. Our room was in the Hilton and overlooked the Pacific Ocean. San Diego events included filming various ads and appearing on radio station interviews to ramp up promotions for the upcoming March of Dimes Superwalk.

We went to the San Diego Zoo in the pouring rain and met a woman there who worked with the animals. She introduced us to some of them. I found peace and serenity in animals. I was naturally drawn to them, perhaps because they could not point to my physical differences. To them, I was just a fellow creature wanting to give them attention and love. And in return, they showed me kindness and love without hesitation or question.

By the end of January, the March of Dimes was already considering new poster children for 1981, and that was the first time that I truly understood this lifestyle wasn't going to last for much longer.

"But you have to think about it this way, Betsy," Mom said. "We'll always have this wonderful year to remember."

Roanoke, Virginia. Philadelphia, Pennsylvania. The trips passed by in a blur, and days and months passed, moving us ever closer to the final days of our tour.

As our year wrapped up, a trip to Morristown, New Jersey, included spending some time with a local first-grade class. It was the first time in all of our travels that I actually felt out of place and self-conscious. Being around unfamiliar children was about the most foreign thing I experienced during that long year. I had grown used to talking to grown-ups and speaking before large audiences. Celebrities and notable figures were child's play. But actual children? I had the acceptance of my friends at school and other children I'd met on tour, but I had no idea how a whole group of my peers would receive me. It turned out that they received me just as well as the children at my own school.

While we were in Morristown, I also took part in a fashion show at the mall. I went on a private tour of Hahn's Department store and got to try on loads of clothes. I was allowed to select three outfits to model. The show itself was so much fun, and I saw Mom in the audience, smiling tearfully at me as I walked down the runway. I felt like a superstar.

Finally, we went to Atlantic City, which was the loudest and most colorful place I'd ever seen. We were picked up from the airport by a police officer, and he gave us a ride to the hotel in his patrol car. I made appearances at the telethon they were hosting there, and then we went to our room. True to the spirit of Atlantic City, it was as unusual a room as we had seen so far. The bed was round, and there was a sunken tub in the bathroom. In our final days in Atlantic City, I met Lou Rawls and presented him with roses on stage before 1,800 people.

We left in the afternoon for Las Vegas, which was blistering hot even in the spring. We were in town for the National Association of Broadcasters Convention—a gathering of over six thousand people. To my eyes, Las Vegas was a magnified version of Atlantic City, and the lights and noise and people stretched for miles without end. Our room was at Caesar's Palace, and it was a riot: all red and purple. There were two beds with mirrors overhead on the ceilings and purple couches. The walls were red velvet, and I thought it was just about the most beautiful and extravagant thing I'd ever seen. I participated in some promotional events, but the real highlight of Las Vegas for me was swimming in the pool itself.

Before we knew it, summer arrived, and with it came the final months of our tour. A new national poster child had been selected and was waiting in the wings. Mom and I felt like we were an old hat at touring now, and it was funny to think back on our early days and how unprepared we'd felt when meeting Melanie and her mom as I transitioned into my role.

By the middle of June, it was beginning to look and feel like the end of our long journey. In Detroit, we went to the Volunteer Leaders Conference, which was a huge March of Dimes event held every four years. By this time, we knew so many of the faces there, whether local chapter leaders or regional and national directors. They all knew me and talked with me as old friends.

At long last, in the first week of August, we found ourselves in Los Angeles, kicking off our last round of travels. Dad went with us this time. So many of the March of Dimes representatives were new; it hardly felt the same.

And then, without so much fanfare and glamor, it was all over. Our last flight was to Louisville, Kentucky, where we met the new, 1981 March of Dimes poster child, Missy. It was not just the end for us but for Nancy as well, as she was retiring from her travelling position.

It was the end for the March of Dimes itself. After my stint as national poster child, Missy was the last national poster child selected before the March of Dimes discontinued the practice. I consider it a blessing to have been one of the last children to represent the March of Dimes on their mission during the 1979–1981 years.

One of the great things we did was meet a lot of kids with disabilities. It was incredible to see how many children out there had been affected by a myriad of birth defects but still managed to be positive and live life fully. Mom found these visits to be the most meaningful, and I think it was good for both of us to see that even though our situation felt so unique and difficult at times, we were not alone.

It was a lovely, easy culmination to what had been an amazing year, and when I was there, in the moment, I had no idea how instrumental those events would be in forming the person I would later become. I was a happy child and grateful for the opportunities that I'd been given. I was prepared, at such an early age, to meet my future with fortitude, faith, and above all, hope.

17
All the Beautiful Lonely Hours

As it does for all of us, time seemed to pass more quickly as I got older. I never quite understood how the national poster child year seemed like a whirlwind for my mom. For me it felt like my time with March of Dimes lasted for ages. It was part of who I was and who I would always be.

After my year as the national poster child, the March of Dimes as we knew it faded away quite significantly. The young girl who came after me was the last poster child the organization had. Things had changed quite a bit from their inception as a polio charity. Again, they were changing with the times, heading in a new direction. Their agenda, along with popular medical understanding, was shifting from a focus on birth defects to the prevention of low birth weight infants and promoting healthy pregnancy behaviors.

Even as we left, we could see the changes taking place within the organization. So, when our time with the March of Dimes was done, it was really over. We didn't stay actively involved, not because we didn't want to but because the people that we'd had connections with had moved on. I moved on too.

The adjustment back into school was relatively easy. I had occasionally made it to the classroom over that year that we were on tour. Mrs. Bryant eased the transition by encouraging me to talk about my experiences on the road and to bring in items I'd received during my travels.

All of my major surgeries had been completed by the time I was six, but there were still maintenance surgeries to be done at irregular intervals. Other than that, I was a healthy child. Mom swore she'd known from the start that there were no other major medical issues involved in my condition, and she was right. I suppose a mother knows these things about her child. The main medical attention I got was from the prosthetists, with whom I was on friendly terms with by that time. Considering how much I was growing through those early years, I had to attend frequent fittings for new prostheses. Every few months or so, I'd start to limp, and that would be the sign that it was time to go in for adjustments. Sometimes, the issue was just that I had played too rough on the leg and had to go in for repair. I still loved to be active.

I advanced at school and made friends. But, gradually, I became more cognizant of the fact that I was different. The source was not external; the realization came from within me. I never experienced bullying. I was surrounded by great people, kind teachers, and caring friends. Despite my fortunate circumstance of having compassionate people around me, there were times I felt the brunt of my own self-struggle. One time in particular was in fifth grade.

It was field day at Allgood Elementary School, an annual spring event held outdoors. Field day consisted of a dozen or more athletic activities that we kids would rotate through all afternoon, competing for bragging rights if not all-out glory. Now, ordinarily this would have been something I'd have loved. I was passionate about physical activity and still loved playing soccer, roller skating, or doing just about anything outside. But that particular day, I just didn't have it in me. Something inside me shut down, and I was convinced that I couldn't participate.

I told myself I wouldn't be good enough. I wasn't as able as the other kids. It would be stupid for me to go out there and make a fool of myself.

I sat inside the classroom alone. I put my head down on the desk and wallowed in the feelings of sadness and rejection. My teacher came into the classroom, having noticed my absence on the field. I'm sure she didn't know what to say. If she did, I wasn't in the mood to hear it anyway. There was less inclusion in schools then than there is now, so it wasn't her fault that she wasn't equipped to know what I was feeling or to support me going out and participating anyway, with or without adaptations.

Finally, she left, and I was entirely alone again. This gave way to a rush of self-pity. Almost all of the field day events included some form of running. It grieved me that I couldn't do everything the way other kids could. Of course, my friends had offered to help me in the three-legged race.

"Come on, Betsy, you can be on our team."

"I'll run with you in the fifty-meter dash, Betsy."

But I didn't want that. In short, I let my self-consciousness get the best of me. And I missed out because of it.

The memory of this experience stayed with me for a long time. There was such a lesson to be learned in it, and I did learn it, eventually. I did not like the feeling of self-defeat, so I learned the only option was to be positive, motivated, and undefeated by self-doubt. It was through this that I learned it was all right to have some moments where there is sadness and struggle, as these experiences can make us stronger and point us in a new, positive direction, if we so allow them. I like to think these lessons treated me well. But throughout the rest of my time in school, most of the struggles I felt were brought on by my own self-consciousness rather than by any outside influence.

There were a few surgeries in my elementary school years; most were scheduled during the summer months so I would not have to miss school. These surgeries were mainly on my leg, and eventually included a procedure to remove the pins and hardware in my right leg, as the bones were now fused. Dr. King's surgeries on my leg were very successful, and he remained prominent in the teaching world of orthopedics. He was well ahead of his time. Dr. King remained head of orthopedics and chief of staff at Georgia Baptist Medical Center in Atlanta for many years, educating many residents in the Brown method that he had performed on me. I like to think because of Dr. King's success with me, he was able to pass along his knowledge to the future orthopedic surgeons, who in turn would help other children born with congenital leg anomalies.

Although not forgotten, the poster child years began to fade slowly away. I began to feel like a normal, healthy child, growing and ever changing. During these changing times, the one constant was my family. At home, I felt beautiful and accepted. Dad was a stickler about getting us to church every Sunday, and we had a close support group of friends around our family at all times. Through the years, Dad travelled quite often with his job. Sara and John were typical siblings, and we laughed, fought, and teased each other. Mom was a wonderful mother to us, but I think we drove her a bit crazy at times. Dad was the disciplinarian, and Mom was the peacekeeper. Dad instilled the fear of God into us and grounded us if we refused to attend church on Sundays. But even then I recognized the values and morals that I was learning, and I was grateful for these.

Past having to get up early for Sunday school, Sundays were actually pretty fun. Some of my best memories were of sitting on Dad's lap in church as a little girl. We always spent the whole day together as a family, having lunch and then Dad would help us with our homework or we'd just all hang out together. Along with church friends, we also had a very tightknit group of neighborhood friends. Many neighbors had kids our ages, and it was not uncommon for evenings to be spent on the street in front of our house playing kickball. Our street was ground zero for all the fun nightly activities, and my dad was the neighborhood dad. He encouraged unity of the kids and neighbors, despite our age or physical differences. He would form and lead the teams. He played pitcher, referee, and coach and felt very comfortable in his roles. We kids loved how his spirit cheered us on, as he never picked sides but assisted and encouraged everyone to be involved. It was a time full of warm memories.

It was also a time of spending summers and holidays with my extended family. Every summer we went to Jackson Hole, Wyoming, to visit Aunt Adele and her family at the summer home they had there. I loved the time our families spent together, and as I grew older, Aunt Adele became like a second mother to me. As Mom's sister, she was very much like my mother but also different enough that I could talk to her about things I wasn't always comfortable talking to Mom about. It was nice having another person outside of my immediate family to share thoughts and

Mom and Aunt Adele

feelings with and to provide a different perspective.

Aunt Adele was a beautiful, graceful woman, inside and out. She carried herself well and was always calm. I never saw her angry. She was very similar to her mother, my Gran. Both were lovely women and very humble. Aunt Adele was a nurse in Shreveport, Louisiana. The home in Jackson Hole was a vacation spot, so our time there always felt idyllic. Like Gran, Aunt Adele always encouraged me and showed me unconditional love. She was less emotional about my physical struggles than Mom, who had experienced the difficulties alongside me and who I felt would always carry some guilt—no matter how unfounded—for my condition.

I was very close to my extended family on my mom's side. I realize now it is because there was such unconditional love and acceptance from Gran and her side of the family. I never had a grandfather I remembered, as my dad's father passed away when he was young and my mom's father passed away when I was not quite two years old. My mom always shared with me the love her father had for me, and she told me the story many times about how he had fulfilled his dream of living to see me walk. I always longed to have a grandfather in my life, but I do feel my mom's father has been with me throughout my life.

As for my grandmother, I feel Gran loved me even more because of the physical differences I was given. The memories of visiting her house in Florida as a young girl have remained with me, and I often reminisce about those days, how I was drawn to the vanity in her bedroom. It was the center of femininity in the room she had once shared with my grandfather. I would sit in front of the mirror on the little stool and draw her scarves out of the drawer one by one, tying them around my shoulders, neck, and hair. She would smile and laugh when I danced across the room in her finery, always encouraging me to explore and experience and engage.

Me and Gran

I was devastated when Gran passed away when I was in sixth grade and left me with nothing more than the memory of that connection we shared. Even though the time with her was short, death could not break our connection. Of course I wanted more time with her, but with a love such as hers for me, it was more than I could ever ask for. Her spirit has always been around me through this life, giving me strength and hope, especially in times of struggle.

Elementary school flew by, and I was becoming older and more mature, a good student by definition, not one to cause any trouble. I always took pride in making good grades and being overall well-rounded. I was looking forward to middle school and making new friends. The school system in those days was very different from today. My elementary school included first through seventh grade, the middle school was eighth and ninth grades, and high school was tenth through twelfth grades. In seventh grade, I tried out to be a local football league cheerleader, and I made the team.

Belonging to the team only added another component of normalcy to my life. It was a time of building confidence and reminding me I could do anything if I tried. I made many friends, some of which I would go through high school with. It was an age of innocence for me, one I would look back on with much appreciation. It was a time where my family was still a huge support system for me. My siblings were finishing their last couple of years in high school and applying to various colleges. I knew I was going to be without them over the next few years as they went away to college, but I could not have anticipated what an impact this would have on our family.

I was also unaware, at that time, of the fragility of my parents' marriage. It had been secretly crumbling for years. The truth would be brought to light over the next few years, and in that time I would feel truly alone without my siblings.

I attended Miller Grove Middle School in Stone Mountain, Georgia, and along with middle school came new insecurities and pressures over being slightly different. However, the teachers and coaches I encountered along the way were very supportive.

It was during my freshman year in middle school that I met Steven. An instant friend, he'd been diagnosed at an early age with rheumatoid arthritis. We bonded over the fact that despite the opportunities we had, we always felt a little bit different compared to others. Steven was a year ahead of me in school, but we became fast, forever friends. He was a huge support to me not only in high school but throughout my later life. It was refreshing to have someone in my life who understood what I was feeling and going through.

Despite the difficulties he himself faced, Steven never used his diagnosis as an excuse to quit anything. Together, we pushed each other to be our best. We would talk for great lengths of time on the phone at night, just being there for each other. We hung out on weekends, went to church, made good grades, and carried on.

"At least when we're together, we can ignore those things that make us different," Steven said.

He helped me see, during that time in my life, that people are basically good.

Bonded by the simple fact of our physical differences and our love and support for each other, our bond only grew stronger as we both experienced intense family dysfunctions. Someone who suffered immense emotional pain early on from his own family tragedies, Steven was my sole ally in my own family struggles.

I've always believed people are brought into our lives for a reason, and this was no exception. To still find the good in people was a remarkable trait Steven possessed during not only our childhood but as he grew into adulthood.

During high school, I chose to focus on my grades rather than on organized sports. I felt that I was surrounded with good people and never associated with any particular clique. I hung out with people from many different groups, and I think this stemmed from the fact that I was uncomfortable with being labeled myself. I understood that we are all different, and I respected all of my classmates for who they were. I went to school activities and Friday night football games just like everyone else, and I was motivated to get good grades and do well.

One of the things that stemmed from my years of exposure to medical care was a desire to be healthy. Perhaps this was to compensate for the physical difficulties I faced. I felt somehow that being as healthy as I could be would make my life easier. And in many ways it did. Even though I wasn't involved in high school sports, I exercised on my own and found it natural to motivate myself. Mom asked me once why I did everything on my own.

"I don't know," I said. "I'm just more comfortable that way."

At the time, she looked a little bit sad, possibly feeling that old guilt again and worrying that I was missing out. But I never felt that I was. And I hope she understood that my habits also stemmed from independence.

I still loved to swim, and I did so as often as I could, but that too was a solo activity. I found peace in that. It may be that it was simply easier to push myself from within than to put myself out there. Regardless, I was okay with things the way they were.

When John and Sara went away to college, our Sunday traditions slowly faded. I was the youngest by five years, so there were many years when it was just Mom, Dad, and me. And when Dad was away on business trips, it was often just Mom and me together. During high school, I tried not to notice the obvious rift that had somehow grown between my parents.

But by the time I was approaching high school graduation, I hardly recognized my family. It got to the point that the times when Mom and I were alone were the most peaceful because it meant there were no closed doors, no fighting between her and my father. Looking back, I began to realize that it had been a long time since I'd seen any affection between my parents.

The problems had really started much earlier than I'd thought. The good years of our family being happy together had begun to diminish after I was about ten years old. Now, I was able to clearly see the unhappiness that surrounded my parents whenever they were together. They slept in different bedrooms. Even when my father was home, he wasn't really there. Sara and John, living away at college, didn't experience the gradual dissolution as keenly as I did.

When my parents divorced after I graduated from high school, it hit us all hard and in very different ways. But what it came down to was that the divorce completely ripped our family apart. It's difficult for children, no matter how old, to reconcile the dissolution of their parents' marriage. Blame is bound to be placed; loyalties are bound to be tested.

As my parents' separation drew nearer, I couldn't understand the actions that precipitated it. The behaviors of my father in particular seemed completely alien to who I had known him to be all my life. At that time in my life, I hardly knew who I was, and it was difficult to face the additional challenge of trying to understand who my parents were.

Toward the finality of my parents' separation, I was still living at home. My mom had remained strong all along, but in the end she broke down and told me things my dad was doing. She had asked him to go to counseling and try to repair what had been broken, but he was cold and told her he didn't want to try anymore. And all of a sudden we were on our own. My mom and I had always been close. We'd forged a bond early—one that couldn't be broken, but there I was without a father and her without a husband.

All those years together as a family were lost in what felt like the blink of an eye. Ultimately, I felt my father was a hypocrite. All those years he'd held himself up as a God-fearing man, staunchly moral. But he broke that moral code in the end, leaving me unmoored as far as my attachment to my faith went. This distance between me and my siblings grew as well, because they hadn't seen what I'd seen and didn't know what I knew.

18

A Similarity in Differences

I slowed, but I did not stop. People passed me as I navigated the steep incline, and now I looked around, calculating the distance I had yet to go, judging how far I'd come. And then I noticed the smiles and nods as people passed.

"Keep it up!"

"You're doing great. Almost there!"

Tears sprang unbidden to my eyes. It suddenly struck me that I was doing this. I was actually doing it. I hadn't been able to run before, and now here I was accomplishing this seemingly impossible goal I'd set for myself. The comments continued to come from well-meaning runners until nine out of ten people who passed offered some sort of encouragement. This fueled me, and I picked up my pace, running among them and feeling my own courage being kindled back to life by the inspiration and goodness offered by everyone around me.

This was, I knew, exactly where I was supposed to be. I had come full circle. When you're born slightly different or not "normal," it makes life more challenging, and you have the choice to either be defeated by what you've been given or turn it around and make it something rewarding. Growing up, I always felt different, but I was saved by my environment. My mom told me I could do whatever I wanted. She didn't set limitations. She let me go out there and try to live as normal a life as I could. If I couldn't do something the way everyone else was doing it, I would learn my own way of doing it. I adapted. We all have this choice, but for some of us it's more a matter of survival than for others, though all of us are made stronger when we choose to overcome.

As this fire in me burned and fueled my desire to make it up the steep incline, I thought back to other struggles I had overcome.

19

Amidst the Light and the Dark

The things that stood out to me were the early days of my medical care, lying on the cold metal X-ray table and feeling scared. It was these times I remembered feeling helpless and afraid. It was a slow evolution, but I recognized that I could turn those negative experiences into something beneficial. In another regard, I wanted to give back to all of the wonderful nurses and doctors I'd been blessed with back when I was a "hospital kid." After I graduated and while still living at home with Mom, I attended a two-year program that was run through the nearby teaching hospital, Atlanta Medical. In 1995, I came out of the program a registered radiologic technologist.

It wasn't long before I was working in orthopedics, helping to make other people's experiences a little better, hopefully, than mine had been as a child. It was a truly rewarding experience.

I still pursued my own health and wellness in my spare time and began to push myself harder in swimming. I loved it as a sport because the water was forgiving of my physical differences and easy on the body. I felt that I could be good at it, and this stimulated that old, familiar desire within me to overcome. Without any particular goal in mind, I dedicated myself wholeheartedly to this new pursuit. I got involved in a swim group in

Atlanta for disabled swimmers. I practiced every day on my own, and when I felt I was ready, I entered myself into a local swim competition. Unlike almost all of the other swimmers, I didn't have a coach going into the meet, but that didn't daunt me. I wanted to prove to myself what I could do.

I ended up getting good times that day and felt proud of the accomplishment. After the meet, a coach approached me and asked me about my training. When he found out I didn't have a coach, he offered to take me on. I was feeling bold and ready to take that next step. After work each day, I swam and trained with the able-bodied Dynamo Swim Club in Atlanta for two hours. My strokes improved rapidly, as did my times, and soon he was entering me into swim meets where I was racing against other disabled swimmers.

After a few years, I'd risen through the local championship ranks to the US National Championship for disabled swimmers. The event was to be held in Minnesota, and my times would determine if I would move on to the Paralympic trials.

When the day arrived, I was as nervous as could be. I'd never been a very competitive person, as I'd always strived more for my own personal best, so meets always gave me butterflies. While I was waiting for my event, I chatted anxiously with some of the other swimmers and met a woman named Nancy.

"You notice how young all these other swimmers are?" she asked me.

I nodded and smiled self-consciously.

"Just think how good they'll be when they get to be our age." She winked.

It was this spark of positivity that drew me to Nancy. We hit it off right away, and I learned that she had a connective tissue disorder called Ehlers-Danlos Syndrome, an auto-immune disorder that attacks joints and blood vessel walls and was gradually debilitating her. More than anything, I admired her tenacity and her sheer will to overcome the disease that threatened her life. She was passionate about swimming, and her enthusiasm was contagious. That was

Me and Nancy, US national Championship, Minnesota.

the beginning of what would become a long and inspiring friendship.

US Swimming, just like many official organizations, has unfortunate politics that go along with it. No one had heard of me when I arrived on the national swim scene that year. The officials had already picked their prize swimmers for the Paralympics, and I shook up the mold they were looking for. There are different ranks for the various disabilities of swimmers, and I was placed in a different category when arriving in Minnesota, one that would require faster times to qualify for the Paralympics. It was disappointing when my times that week weren't enough to qualify me, but the experience was priceless.

Despite not making it past the national championships, I still felt that I had overcome a great hurdle. I stayed on the swim team in Atlanta and continued to train, never feeling that I had to push myself too hard. I participated in some local competitions, but I placed little pressure on myself to succeed. I swam for fitness and for myself. It was the best motivator of all; however, Nancy was motivating me to aim for the next Paralympics in four years. She was furious about the decisions that were made in Minnesota, about my times and the rank I was put in.

Nancy and I would go through many hurdles together, supporting each other and motivating each other along the way. It was more than swimming that bonded us. It was life and the tragedies of life we would experience over the next decade together. She would be my maid of honor at my wedding and then my best friend through the divorce. She would inspire me to keep going when I felt like giving up. It was a unique friendship that existed over many miles as she was living in New York and I was in Georgia. There were many phone calls with conversations lasting for hours. Unlike me where my surgeries were done in my early years, she would need surgeries often due to her tissues breaking down in her knees, shoulders, and even in her chest. She still managed to swim and train in between her surgeries. Nancy was always a true motivator and inspiration to me.

I was in my twenties and working for an orthopedic practice in Atlanta. Single, I enjoyed life and was blessed with a good job. I dated like most twenty-somethings and usually did not have a hard time meeting people. I was blessed with people who accepted and loved me, and in return, I grew from those relationships. I had a townhome in Duluth, Georgia, and eventually bought a house. It was an innocent time for me. I thrived on my independence and was still learning who I was through life lessons.

I continued to swim and work out at a local gym in the area. I found much joy in step aerobics and was a regular in the class. I became friends with many people at the gym, and I felt safe in this environment. I felt accepted by the people there and found comfort in their stated admiration for my desire to work out and exercise. I was not afraid to take first row in front of the aerobic classes. I felt I could give back to others and hopefully inspire someone along the way. I was not afraid of who I was, and it was a time of growth and much joy for me.

Even in those joys, I felt I was missing something in my life. I had been through a few long-term relationships with wonderful people, but something was missing. I was thirty now and wanted to find someone to share my life with. I had a great decade of being single and growing, both professionally and personally.

I enjoyed my job as an X-ray technologist at the orthopedic office, but I started taking some classes on the side in preparation for nursing school one day. There was always a desire deep within me to become a nurse so I could give back to all those wonderful nurses who'd cared for me as a child. I let my desires be known to the universe, and some days I was short on patience. I could only see that I was getting older, not realizing I was on my journey and everything happened in the time it was supposed to.

In my frustrations and through the trials and tribulations, I would turn to my mom and alternatively to Aunt Adele, who always offered that untainted perspective I needed. Aunt Adele had been diagnosed with breast cancer around that time but had undergone treatment and was then in remission. Her own health struggles were the cause of much worry for Mom and me, but they also drew the three of us even closer together. For many years, my aunt was a sounding board for me while I dated and finally met a man I wanted to spend the rest of my life with.

I met him on a website, one that was known for more long-term relationships, not just a random hookup. I was scared, but I knew others who had met their spouses online. It was 2005, and the Internet dating world was exploding. Growing short on patience from not meeting anyone locally, I decided to give it a try. I met a few people online, not really feeling a connection or having much luck. An e-mail here or there but overall nothing to write home about.

Then, one day I received an e-mail from a man in West Virginia. He was single with a son, a previous failed marriage, and was very open about his life. He was looking for someone to share his life with. *West Virginia? Where the crap is that? Up north somewhere,* I thought to myself, embarrassed by not really knowing. E-mails led to phone calls and more phone calls. We began to talk every day, and he knew about my physical differences. I felt I could share anything with him. We continued to talk for weeks, and then weeks turned into a couple of months.

We were growing tired of telephone calls and curious about meeting in person. We decided to meet one weekend halfway between our respective homes. I felt I knew him pretty well but made sure my friends knew where I was going to be. I would not tell my mom until after the fact, as I knew she would not be happy about my decision to drive somewhere to meet a man I had never met before. It was pretty ballsy on my behalf if not downright dangerous.

It turned out to be a wonderful weekend and a start to a long-distance relationship. We took turns visiting each other. It was six hours from Atlanta to Beckley, West Virginia, where we would cram in weekend trips and any time off from our jobs. Things were moving fast; it had been only five months when he asked me to marry him. I was caught up in the moment of being in love, not able to see anything else in front of me, especially the red flags.

We married when I was thirty-two years old. I resigned from my orthopedic job of ten years and moved to West Virginia. Work was impossible to find, and I struggled to find a job. I was desperate to find work and took a job as a front office assistant in a physical therapy office. It was very humbling, as I was not utilizing any of my radiology skills and was making less than half of what my salary had been.

In my new position, I became fast friends with one of the physical therapists, Lisa. I found much joy in our friendship, as I had no friends in this strange new world. I was struggling to find happiness in this time of my life and realized I still had so much to learn. I thought I had the world all figured out, but reality was starting to set in. I felt alone and isolated in my new surroundings. I had no family near me, a job I did not like, a stepson I was trying to get to know and a family to blend into, and one friend. I became lost and depressed, and my husband became impatient and angry. It was at this time I realized my husband was not who I thought he was.

I did love him but found it difficult fitting into his lifestyle. Fighting became a regular occurrence, followed by making up—a vicious circle we drew over and over. Many nights I would be at home in tears after he squealed out of the driveway in his truck after a fight. My mom was distant in my life, as the wedding had caused even more of a rift in my family; it was my doing that caused this distance. Trying to reconnect with my father, I invited him and his new wife to the wedding only a couple of months before. It was a poor decision on my behalf, as this caused much pain for my mom. As many nights were spent in tears, I had time to reflect on these incidences and only hoped the relationship between my mom and me could be repaired.

In the meantime, I only did what I had to—pull myself up like I had done my whole life. I was not going to be defeated by this current situation. I continued to work at the therapy office but also found a YMCA and started swimming. For it was in swimming I had always found a reprieve. It was also during this time I started to teach step aerobics at a local gym. It was a big step for me to get in front of a class and teach people, but I was quickly rewarded. I was constantly told how motivational it was for others to see me up there doing what they had doubted they could do themselves. It lifted me up a little, to think that I could be an inspiration to others just by putting myself out there in a way that I may not normally be comfortable with. I felt as if I was getting back on track but later realized I was only pushing unresolved issues further down inside of my subconscious.

My husband took a job in Roanoke, Virginia, and we

relocated to this town. It was a much-needed move, and I felt a new beginning for us. I found work in an orthopedic office as an X-ray technologist and was happy to be doing work in my field. I enjoyed my work and made friends with my coworkers. I felt this was a turning point, not only in my new marriage but also for me.

Life went on, and I was still on my journey of self-actualization. I had no idea then what I would have to endure through the process, but I was eager to find out who I was and how to put forward the best I had to offer. Then, after two years of marriage, when I was thirty-four, I found out that I was pregnant. I was elated. I had grown up with wonderful women as role models, and I wanted to be that light in my child's life. Despite our marital difficulties, the idea of new life seemed to give my husband and me hope and brighten our days. Anything was surmountable after all. But even then there was a glimmer of apprehension.

Of course I had always wondered if my condition was something that I would risk passing on to my children. But I'd always been healthy, and no one really knew what had caused my birth defects. I was never told not to try to have children, and when I did ask my doctor, he said he agreed that I was in good health with no family history of birth defects; there was nothing wrong with trying. The future was wide open, and I was going to bring a new life into it and be the mother I'd always dreamed of being.

I took my prenatal vitamins with religious regularity. What we now knew about folic acid and the prevention of birth defects was due in large part to efforts on behalf of organizations like the March of Dimes. How beautifully ironic that my child could now benefit from these things.

At first, everything went smoothly. Because of my own condition, my doctor wanted me to come in a little more regularly for ultrasounds, but he assured me this was just a routine precaution. It was early yet, and the baby was growing. Weeks passed—six weeks, eight weeks, ten. And then I went in one day, and the doctor took longer than normal analyzing the images on the monitor. A crease formed between his eyes. Try as I might to stare at the fuzzy images on the screen, I could make no sense of what he saw or the cause of what I was now sure was concern on his face.

"Well, I've been going over the measurements here, and I'm not seeing what I'd like to be seeing," he said.

Suddenly, my mind was filled with questions. *What measurements? What does it mean? Surely the fragile thump of the heartbeat I hear means everything is all right?*

The doctor wiped the jelly from my stomach with a cloth and replaced the ultrasound sensor.

"I want you to get dressed, and I'll come back in to talk with you about what we're dealing with here, okay?"

A pat on the arm told me that it wasn't going to be something I wanted to hear. My stomach dropped, and I fought the tears back.

I can do this, I thought. *I can be ready for anything. I can love this baby and raise this baby no matter what; just let it be healthy. Please, just let it be healthy.*

Everything changed that day. The baby was not healthy. "Not thriving" were the words the doctor used, and those two words hung in my mind and would not go away. The ultrasound indicated the presence of numerous deformities. So numerous that they were interfering with life itself. The baby's growth had slowed. There was talk of the vital systems, the lack of proper functioning, the failure to sustain life. And what it came down to were two options. Wait and watch the baby waste away, or terminate the pregnancy. My doctor heavily recommended the latter.

"I would never make a suggestion of this magnitude lightly," he said. "Of course it's ultimately your decision ..."

And so the most difficult choice I'd faced in my entire life was laid before me.

Either possibility was too hard to fathom. I could hardly

think. I could hardly breathe. I wanted to leave and never come back. I wanted to go back in time to when everything was all right.

We terminated the pregnancy at thirteen weeks. I was in an agony of guilt and despair. I had always believed in life, and I believed in the life inside of me. I loved it. But I also believed in peace and well-being for that tiny life.

When it was over, I was bereft. It all felt like such a cruel and horrible waste. I felt no peace, no well-being. But I had to believe that I had made the right decision. Even then, I knew I would never be without grief for what I'd lost.

Afterward, it became essential that we find the answers to the many questions. *Why did this happen?* Doctors became interested in the case, and I began to undergo a series of DNA tests. Every appointment was prefaced with questions, and every conversation was punctuated with references to genetic studies. None of the news was positive. And finally I was delivered with a final, crushing blow. The traits I possessed—those that caused my own deformities—were autosomal dominant. It was the worst kind of genetic anomaly. The chances of my ever having healthy children were extremely low.

The following weeks and months were spent processing this news. My husband and I both dealt with it in our own ways. As grief will do, our own private struggles caused a rift in our marriage that was almost impossible to overcome. I was devastated not only by the loss of the child I had carried but for the loss of any future children I might have had. I knew now that I would not have children of my own. I wouldn't go through the agony of propagating a life that may or may not be able to sustain itself. I couldn't go through the horror again of having to choose to terminate that life. For me, everything I knew ended with the loss of that tiny spark of hope, including my will to put the last of my efforts toward my crumbling marriage.

At last there was nothing left to do but try to put it all

behind me. Aunt Adele had always said, "Go with the resistance." Sometimes it was necessary to take the hard road in order to come out stronger on the other side. These words could not have rung truer, as I was realizing my thirties were going to be some of the most difficult years of my life.

Along with the grief of my failing marriage and loss of my baby and the potential of ever becoming a mother, I learned Aunt Adele's breast cancer had returned. This time, the disease spread quickly, and there was nothing to be done. None of us were ready to say good-bye. Throughout her illness, she often repeated her same mantra of "Go with the resistance." She never did what was easy. She fought for her life, but she also handled her defeat with grace. When she finally passed, my mom was with her. The news came as a blow, and I mourned for another loss. It was a particularly difficult time in my own life and marriage, but just as I had always felt Gran around me, I knew that Aunt Adele's spirit would be with me always.

20
Life after Karma

When we divorced, it was a time of grieving for me. The loss of not being able to have any children was painful enough, and to now grieve the loss of a marriage, a stepson, and in-laws was almost too much to bear. The end was much of my own doing; choices I made forever haunt me, and it will always be with much regret. I know now that if I had truly known myself, I would have done things differently; I would not have hurt the ones I loved and would have quite possibly chosen a different course.

Although it was a lot of me that caused the demise of my marriage, I cannot accept all the blame. My husband refused to hear my cries and calls for help. Grief and denial can lead us to poor choices, choices that have forever consequences.

I knew I couldn't do the kind of soul searching I needed to do while dragging another unhappy life along with me. I moved out on my own, bought a little house on the side of a mountain, right in the middle of nature, and I never felt more alone. I tried to find solace in walks through the woods and along mountain streams, but nothing could take the pain away. I would learn that the pain would eventually become more tolerable, but it would never completely go away. I missed my husband, being married, my stepson, and I knew I would never have them again. It was a terrible loss. My father showed no support for me, my mom was very distant, and my siblings were absent from my life. I was completely alone.

One particular day on my daily walk in nature by the mountain stream close to my house, I carried a couple of seashells in my hand. They held precious memories of the past few years. One was a conk shell, beautiful with pink and white colors throughout, now broken. I remembered the moment my husband retrieved it from the bottom of the ocean on our honeymoon just a few years before. I held it close to my heart as I continued my walk. Just as the water in the mountain stream was flowing swiftly, the tears flowed down my face. I remembered back to when the shell was broken as he threw it on the tile. It was the day I moved out of the house. It was one of my favorite gifts; I watched as he angrily picked it up from the ledge in the bathroom it was sitting on and, without hesitation, threw it to the ground. I had grabbed the broken pieces from the floor and ran out of the house. It was symbolic of what our marriage had become, broken and in pieces. It would be flashbacks of images like these that would haunt me many times.

As I came back into the present moment, I turned to the water in the stream and found a place on the bank to sit. It was time to let this particular incident go, and I thought the best way was to give the shells back to the earth. The other shell was one we retrieved together on one of his fishing trips to the outer banks. It was similar to a conk-type shell but was gray in color with circular patterns throughout. I looked at these shells and remembered the good times we experienced, trying to process the mess it became. I gently set the shells in the stream; the water was shallow, and they sat on the bottom of the creek bed. I watched the water flow over them, and I hoped the water took all the anger, hurt, and pain with it and washed them clean. I sat there for a long while on the bank and tried to make peace with my situation. How I wished the water from the stream could wash away the pain and grief from inside of me. I would come to realize it would take many years for the pain to go away. I could feel the love of the earth around me as I sat on the bank.

It was growing dusk, and I needed to get home before dark. I looked at my precious shells one last time as they sat in their new home on the bed of the stream. I said good-bye and slowly turned to begin my walk home.

In Virginia, I had a career and coworkers I liked. I was thankful for those things, and it is what helped me move forward in my dark moments of grief. I had been in the medical field for twelve years and had worked closely with doctors. I was thirty-five and decided I needed to start over. After much loss, I wanted to make a change. I had always wondered if nursing would be more rewarding and give me a closer relationship with patients, allowing me to provide them with a higher level of care. That's what I wanted. I wanted to make a difference in people's lives.

So, I went back to school and earned my nursing degree from a community college in Roanoke, Virginia. Because of my experience and the associate's degree I'd already obtained in radiology, I was able to finish my RN requirements in a year and a half. Once I graduated, I worked in Virginia, specializing in adult medicine and cardiac care. I worked in a progressive care unit. The work was rewarding, I loved my house, and yet I still knew that there was something missing in my life. I began to realize that if I really wanted to start over, I might have to do it somewhere else. It was hard for me to think of leaving Virginia; I'd made a home there. But it was equally nerve-wracking, given how small the town was, to consider every time I went to the grocery store that I might run into my ex-husband or his parents.

I began considering my options. I thought about moving back to Georgia, where I'd grown up, but it didn't feel like the right thing to do. I needed a blank slate. I began looking for open nursing positions and landed on a position in Charleston, South Carolina. I'd always loved the South, and Charleston had that old romantic charm that I might enjoy. I interviewed for the position over the phone, and then I drove down to interview in person, and I was basically hired the same day. Of course it was exhilarating, but part of me wondered what I had done in accepting a job in a place where I knew no one.

At that point in my life, I only had a few acquaintances in Virginia, and I didn't feel like I knew where my home was. It was difficult to make the decision to move, but I was eager for my new life to begin.

As I packed my house up for the move south, I also spent many days in the woods around my mountain home. I was preparing for my good-bye, and it was very difficult. I had grown accustomed to seeing deer, fox, bears, and even coyotes around the house, and I loved it. I had quite a bird population around me as well. It was still cold in February when I left, and I was worried about the birds having food until spring. I bought enough feeders to spread around throughout the woods. It was my way of saying thank you and good-bye. The nature of this place had served me well and helped me heal. I was sad to leave it but knew if I was ever going to get over my husband, I would have to leave Virginia. As I placed the feeders in random trees, I said a blessing for all of the living creatures around me and prayed for their safety and survival.

The transition in Charleston was difficult. I longed for being back in Virginia and wondered if I had made the right decision in moving. I was still processing the loss of my marriage and the reality of never being able to have children. I began dating someone, someone I had known since elementary school, but even I knew it was too soon. I was not over the pain of my previous losses. As time will resolve many things, that relationship dissolved as it should have. It would be hard to have a healthy relationship with anyone as I was still thinking about my previous life with my ex-husband.

I thought back many times to the divorce and what I could

have done differently. I thought back to Virginia and how my ex-husband had wanted to work things out and get help; I refused. A decision I would often debate in my head over the years. Deep down, I knew it was not an option for me to return to Virginia. I had heard my ex-husband had remarried and moved on with his life. It was a bittersweet moment as I always clung to a little hope that maybe one day things would be different.

When I heard of his remarriage, the finality rang clear in my head. Here I was in another state, still hoping one day there may be reconciliation between us. My unrealistic hopes were shattered in an instant. It was painful to process, but I only wanted him to be happy. I knew I had to let go of the past mistakes and decisions I made. It was all gone. I had no other choice but to say my final good-byes to the life I had in Virginia as I realized I would never go back there now. I knew I would never forget the valuable lessons I had learned and tried to find solace in the growth I had undergone as a person.

In the ensuing months, I tried to focus more on my job and my work with patients and caring for them. I grew tremendously as a nurse and as a person. I worked with some wonderful nurses, one of whom was a younger woman named Gillian. She'd only been working at the hospital for about six months prior to my arrival. She and I hit it off immediately. She was going through a divorce, and that instantly gave us some common ground. I was fitting in to my new surroundings. I quickly joined a gym and began taking step aerobics classes, and I also began swimming in a nearby recreation facility. It felt nice to exercise and work out again, and it gave me renewed strength, both physically and emotionally. I aligned myself with a new prosthetist in Charleston as well. Steven and his partner, Rhett, were in their early thirties, and I was impressed with how open-minded and progressive they were in their thinking about prosthetics. I felt that they really wanted every patient to experience life to the fullest. I continued to meet people and make a life for myself in Charleston. I met a woman named Tracy who was a life coach, shaman, and energy healer. I started taking therapy with her, and she talked to me about balance and energy. I began to realize that my difficulties ran deeper than I'd thought. I'd been to various therapists in my twenties and thirties for family and self-esteem issues, but it took finding Tracy to lead me to the spiritual path that changed my life. With all of this, I suddenly knew that Charleston was where I was meant to be and that I'd been meant to come here for a reason. All of these people were put into my life for a reason, and I began to recognize how fortunate I was. And all of this was before I even met Eric.

I had lived in Charleston for a year and a half. Tracy and I had been working a lot on healing my energy, and I'd come to experience a sort of spiritual awakening. After everything that had happened with my dad and his total rejection of the moral and religious code he taught us to live by, I had really begun to question organized religion many years earlier. My dad's leaving had confused my beliefs. Since then, my questioning led to me to open my mind to many different beliefs. I came to find over the years that all religions have some basis in truth. There are some people who do horrible things to others in the name of religion, and I believe they'll have to answer to that, but for the most part I believe we are all instruments of love, or should be, as we are all connected. We all have a place in this world, and we should try to come together rather than judge and find others wanting. In reality, we are all wanting, but we are also each perfect in our own way.

My understanding of life in this way was really helping me to grow and understand who I was as a person. Up to this point, I had struggled with self-confidence. I hadn't quite realized how much I was affected by this. Being born different and having family issues when I was younger, and in my adulthood, played against me as far as figuring out who I was. It took me going through what I went through as an adult to realize I was okay being who I was, and I was going to be okay. I had a rewarding career and felt I was giving back in a meaningful way. I had an interesting perspective on nursing from all the time I spent in hospitals during my childhood. I tried to carry that over into my nursing career by being compassionate and empathetic above all else. This, too, helped me grow as an individual.

In my short time in Charleston, I had, for the first time, a truly deep friendship with a wonderful woman. Before I knew it, Gillian and I were best friends. Gillian's friendship was special to me on so many levels, and not simply because it was the first time I had allowed myself to be bonded to a best friend. All my life, I'd hung out on the fringes, forming friendships with everyone I could but never really having a best friend with whom I shared my deepest thoughts and feelings. I began to realize this was because I'd never really trusted myself to open up to another. I never truly believed that people would love me for who I was. Now that I was in a place where I felt comfortable doing that, I was being rewarded for my efforts. In short, I was, for the first time, truly happy with where I was at in my life.

That's when I met Eric. Oddly enough, we met online, which was something I never thought I'd do again. I signed up for a one-week trial, just wanting to dip my toes in the water again. I was quite terrified to go this route again considering the unfortunate outcome of the last online experience with my ex-husband. The age of the Internet was only continuing to grow, and while Charleston was home to many single people, it was so difficult to meet a quality person with common desires and interests. Eric and I were matched up almost immediately.

Eric was a firefighter on Sullivan's Island, which is just off the coast of Charleston. We e-mailed each other and started talking on the phone. I was comfortable with getting to know him that way. He was a nice guy, and it turned out we had a lot in common. But I wasn't sure I trusted the process enough to meet him in person. Besides, then I would have to explain to yet another person about those things that made me different. A month went by. I realized that I was starting to really like this guy. He asked me to meet him for dinner, in person. It was time to make a decision.

Although we had talked frequently on the phone the past month, this was our first date and our first opportunity to meet each other face-to-face. I was so nervous. The conversations over the past few weeks on the phone with him had been easy. We would talk for hours, and we both found reassurance in life just by hearing that voice on the other end of the line. It was a time in my life when I was looking for a lasting, committed relationship. I was growing tired of failed relationships, and it had been about four years since my divorce. I still carried some shame with me about the failure of my marriage but knew inside it was time to let it go.

Eric and I talked about love, life, experiences, family, friends, beliefs, and hopes. We were on the same page about so many things. I found happiness and joy in our phone conversations. I had agreed to the date without sounding hesitant, but inside I was afraid to meet him. I really liked this guy ... but I still had not told him about my leg. I thought, *I have a couple more days before our date. I'll find the right time before then to tell him.*

The next couple of days went by fast; I couldn't quit thinking about the date with Eric, and then the little voice inside of me would surface, raising its doubts. *What if he doesn't want to go out with me after I tell him about my leg?* I pushed that annoying voice back inside as I went shopping for an outfit for the date. I thought if I could just look good enough, he wouldn't even notice my leg. I ended up finding a dress for the date, and when the night came, I was ready. He called me that day to give me directions to his house. We were meeting there first, as it was halfway between my house and the restaurant. I took the directions down, and somewhere in the middle of our good-byes, I took a deep breath and blurted out, "Eric, I have to tell you something, and I'm so sorry I waited until just before our date."

The conversation went quiet.

He finally said, "Okay, I'm here. What is it?"

Deep breath again. "Uh, well ..."

C'mon, Betsy, don't stutter. Just be strong and say it.

"I have a prosthesis on my right leg from the knee down; I was born without a bone in my leg. I am so sorry I didn't tell you before now."

Silence.

And then, "Is that it?" he asked.

"Uh yeah, that's it."

Tell him about the hands later. Just get through this first.

"Okay. You scared me, Betsy. I thought it was going to be something bad. I can't wait to see you in a little bit."

"Okay, I'll see you shortly," I stuttered.

Hanging up the phone, I wondered if it could really be that easy. I realized later it really was.

The drive to his house was interesting. My mind was constantly analyzing the previous conversation. *Did he hear what I said? Is he really that accepting? Is he going to be gone when I get there?* So many questions. I kept getting closer to the address, my stomach full of butterflies.

When I arrived, I sat in my car for a moment and just continued to take deep breaths. *It will be okay*, I told myself. *I should be more worried about just going over to the house of a guy I've never met.* But I felt in my heart that he was a good person—a firefighter in his working life, saving others. I felt the universe was on my side right now and had led me to the front door of this house to meet this particular person.

Another deep breath. Then I knocked.

I heard some stirring in the house, my nerves about to explode.

There was some fumbling with the door, and then it opened. Our eyes locked together, and in an instant there was a connection so deep, it felt like a lightning bolt had just struck both of us simultaneously. This energy travelled from both of our hearts and connected somewhere in the middle. It was all in a look. All my fears and nerves were immediately calmed. There was nothing else in that second that mattered. Nothing but us.

The night was amazing as we had dinner in downtown Charleston. Conversation was still easy and flowed without much thought; it was just the two of us laughing and talking. We had no idea in that moment how our relationship would grow and that we would experience so much love over the coming months. We had no idea we would be married in a little over a year. But everything felt good and right, and I didn't want it to end.

After dinner, we decided to take a walk on the boardwalk by the Charleston harbor. Charleston, with all its history and beauty, is amazing in itself. There is a street in Charleston where elegant houses are located along the harbor called the Battery. These houses are the most historic in the area and are worth millions of dollars. They are the homes that have been passed down from old money and have belonged to the most prominent families in the history of Charleston.

The August night was warm, but the breeze off the harbor was refreshing. Eric and I walked hand in hand that night on the Battery. The water splashed below us on the rocks, and as I looked out over the water, the moon—not quite full—was reflecting off the surface. The love and bond Eric and I had already formed filled me entirely. It was a beautiful moment. We continued to walk and talk, not fully understanding the deep connection we had with one another but gladly accepting this feeling of love. As I looked at the moon, seeing the brightness in its glory and hearing the water splash below, I said thanks to the universe and to whatever power had led me to this point. I was finally where I was supposed to be.

Before our first date ended, Eric had already asked if he could see me the following day. We dated regularly after that, and every time we went out, he would line up our next date. I had little room to doubt his feelings for me, and I reveled in it. It felt surreal to be adored so completely. Our friendship continued to grow along with our romantic feelings toward one another, and we talked and talked, telling each other anything and everything. I felt comfortable and safe with him, knowing that my physical differences didn't matter to him at all. He didn't see them when he looked at me.

As summer turned to fall, I began to hear talk at work of the annual Bridge Run that was held in April of every year. I mentioned it to Eric.

"It's silly I guess, but I've always thought it would be so great to just be able to run like that, without stopping. I've never been able to do that. I think someday I'd like to."

"That's not silly at all. You should do it. If you want to, I mean. I could help you train for it."

The more I thought about it, the more I realized it really was something I wanted to do. I'd overcome so many things in my life by sheer force of will. Why not this? And I had an amazing man by my side who was offering to go the distance with me. His encouragement was essential, as it turned out.

The training was long and difficult. Eric had been a wrestler in college and was a firefighter—athletic and well trained. He was good at motivating me and keeping me accountable, but I also had that same internal drive in me that kept me going. I had nine months in which to prepare myself. When I first hit the track, I couldn't run fifty yards without stopping.

"Okay," Eric said. "We have our work cut out for us. But just think how good you'll feel when you cross that finish line." And he swept me up in a hug that told me I already had it all.

21
Top of the World

My muscles clenched, and my lungs ached, but ahead of me I could see the spot where the bridge leveled. This, too, spurred me forward. A father and son gave me thumbs-up; a woman fell into step beside me momentarily and cheered me on. Everything inside of me burned, but I couldn't stop smiling.

Finally, I reached the pinnacle, and the whole world spread out before me in one slow, dazzling display. And then I knew I could finish this. It was mine. As I was running level on the bridge, I gave a quick glance behind me to look at what I had just accomplished. Looking

Running up incline of bridge with others behind me

187

ahead, I could see for miles all around me, and the Charleston harbor looked beautiful in all its glory. There were sailboats and other boats in the harbor, and I wondered if those below were watching as the runners powered across the bridge. I felt so powerful, and my exhaustion fled. I looked out over the bay and looked at those people around me in all directions. Even though I was surrounded by hundreds of individuals, I was in my own small space, looking out over the boats and the sun glinting off of the water in the harbor.

A double-amputee passed me, and he was flying on his running blades. We waved to each other, acknowledging and saluting a thousand untold struggles. And that, I realized, was what we were all doing out there on the bridge: acknowledging a strength and solidarity that comes with *living*.

22
Alignment

Eric knew from the beginning that I wanted to get married. I wasn't at a point in my life where I wanted a long-term boyfriend or live-in partner. I wanted commitment. I wanted to lay down roots and feel the bonds of family. I knew I would never be having kids of my own, and Eric was of the same mind-set. He'd never really wanted to have children. His parents went through a divorce when he was a kid, and he himself had never married. I think it took him a little longer than it took me to process what we had found in each other and to recognize and accept the possibilities for our future together.

It had been a little over a year when, on a cool October morning, Eric nudged me to wake up. We both had the day off together, and I preferred to spend such mornings sleeping in and enjoying my freedom from the jarring reality of an alarm. Being a nurse, my days began with the alarm clock at 5:30 in the morning, and my workday would not end until close to eight at night. My workdays were long, but I loved what I did, and that made it all worth it. I grumbled awake and looked at the clock. Five thirty.

"You've got to wake up," he was saying. "I heard there's a really cool planetary alignment happening. I thought we could go down to the harbor to see it when the sun comes up."

Interesting ... planetary alignment. I haven't heard about this. I thought it was unusual, as I have a love for astronomy, astrology, and everything else regarding the universe.

"You know I don't have to be at work today, right?"

"All the more reason not to waste a minute of the day," he joked. "Come on, Betsy, please? Come with me?"

It was then that I detected the note of urgency in his voice. He was trying to get me out of bed for a reason. Something clicked in my mind. I sat up in bed, trying to clear my head.

"All right. If it means that much to you."

I got up and went into the bathroom, discreetly putting on as much makeup as I could get away with and making sure I didn't have bed head, just in case. *He seems very persistent ... is he going to do it today?* I thought to myself. I had checked my phone app for any planetary alignments today, and there were none. I became excitedly suspicious. I threw on some clothes, warm and cute, as I wanted to look nice for whatever he had in store for me.

He drove me out to a private park by the Charleston Harbor. No one was there. The sun was just starting to come up, and the moon was still overhead. The air had turned crisply cold on this October morning, and the wind off the harbor made it even colder. I zipped my jacket up and snuggled close to him as we walked along the water. It really was beautiful, and I exclaimed at the sight as we walked to the edge of the water. And then he did it. He got down on one knee and asked me to marry him.

I, of course, said yes. As the sunrise was reflecting off the water, the moon shone down on us in all its beauty. I felt this was the planetary alignment Eric spoke of earlier: our planetary alignment. The universe is always providing alignments in our life, and I knew this was part of that greater plan.

Throughout the following year, we were busy with wedding plans. It could not have been an easier process. The fire department Eric worked for provided much support, including the facility for our reception. It was an outdoor facility owned by the fire departments for their various events throughout the year. We spoke with the city, and they approved our ceremony site behind Fort Moultrie only a block away from the reception facility. Everything was lining up perfectly, and the year of planning flew by with tremendous speed.

The week of the wedding included many events for the two of us. Family and friends arrived throughout the week. There was a cocktail party one evening for us, and the rehearsal dinner was at a restaurant on Sullivan's Island. It was a perfect week surrounded by the love of the people who meant the most to me.

The day arrived, October 4, 2014. The morning of the wedding was typical for a bride, busy and exciting. Fortunately, everything was in place, so I sipped on champagne as my mom and a few friends helped me get ready. Thankful my mom and I had repaired our broken relationship over the past few years, I was glad we were close again and she was here with me. My hair and makeup lady came to the house; my photographer was busy catching spur-of-the-moment pictures of me getting ready. I felt relaxed, peaceful, and above all else loved. I relished every second of every moment of this day. It was a perfect day I knew would only happen once. I wanted it to last forever. Everything in my life had led me to this very moment. Every loss, every joy, every decision led me here on my journey. I gave thanks to the universe in all its wonderfulness.

As I slipped on my wedding dress, the simplicity of it was beautiful. The dainty straps and beaded detail on the front, the slightly open back and the train just long enough to feel like a princess. It was all I wanted in a dress, simple but elegant. I could feel the presence of Aunt Adele and Gran around me and knew they were with me. I rode to the fire station with my mom and stepdad and felt an overwhelming calmness. I arrived at the fire station and was attended to by a couple of firefighters Eric worked with. They were very attentive, offering me water, a chair, and holding the train of my dress.

"It's time, Betsy," Curt said. He was the firefighter driving me to the wedding.

They helped me into the fire truck, carefully placing the train of my dress over my lap. I was on my way the meet my future husband. The ride to the wedding site was wonderful. *Remember every second of this. Take in everything you see, feel, and hear. It will only happen at this very second, and then it will be gone.* I absorbed the sight of the bright sun shining above me, the slightly cool air coming into the window, the smells of the island as we drove closer and closer to my destination. Curt turned on the sirens as we arrived at my destination. I could see people standing by the rocks on the site of our ceremony.

As the truck pulled up behind the Fort, Eric's brother, Jason, met me at the door of the truck. Curt and Jason helped me down, and the walk on the sidewalk began. It was an awe-inspiring moment as I looked out through the distance and saw everyone who was waiting for me. The walk from the truck to the ceremony site was probably a few hundred feet. As I walked with Jason, I told him how thankful I was to have him as my brother-in-law. I had lost contact with my own brother years prior when our family was split apart. I was now blessed with a brother who loved me unconditionally, and I held onto his arm even tighter with this thought. Again, another blessing that was bestowed upon me. How could I ever give thanks for all the many gifts I was given?

We continued our walk toward the crowd that was waiting for us. The sidewalk ended, and we stepped on the sandy path leading the way to my future husband. I could now see Eric waiting for me along with those I loved the most around him. Tracy, my shaman and energy healer, was standing next to Eric, as she was performing the ceremony. Upon reaching them, I hugged my brother as he helped me step into the ring of seashells Eric was standing in. The shells were in a circle, signifying the sacredness and completeness of not only the ceremony but our love as well.

Tracy performed a hand-fasting ceremony, an ancient Celtic tradition, which symbolized our commitment and intentions to each other. As the ceremony continued, waves splashed over the rocks as if the earth was giving its approval. In the distance, a

cruise ship was going out to sea, and the masses of people could be seen on the decks of the ship. The ceremony was perfect; not a cloud in the sky, and the sun shone brightly. I relished in the warmth and peace I found in it. We had close to a hundred of our closest friends and family standing around us, including Gillian, Eric's brother and parents, and my mom and stepdad. It was perfect. I could not have imagined a better day.

As we arrived at the reception site, following pictures after the wedding, the feeling of love was overwhelming. Eric and I made our way to the microphone to do a quick speech. As I held the microphone and looked out into the crowd, I was overwhelmed with feelings of gratitude and love. We gave our speeches and toasted to love and life and spent the rest of the reception talking, dancing, drinking, and being thankful for the wonderful

family and friends we had been blessed with. I felt as if everything in my life had come together in a circular, beautiful way.

It was like being on the Bridge Run that day, drawing from
the encouragement and inspiration of others, feeling that inexplicable ebb and flow of energy and inspiration and love. Now,
when I think about
it, I realize I may not
have gotten every-
thing I've wanted
out of my life so far,
but I have every-
thing I need. Family,
I've come to realize,
is what you make
of it. Friends can
become family, and
I'm lucky enough to
have those friends in
my life that I hold in
that regard.

Gillian and Jill
have been amazing
female companions
to my days. In the
years between both
of our divorces,
Gillian and I both met and married wonderful men. It was this
shared experience that helped to forge our bond. Since then, she
and her husband had two little girls. Gillian knew about the
pain I've suffered in longing to be a mother and my grief over
not being able to have children. So I've become an aunt to her
children. In this way, I've been able to open my heart to the love
that children bring, even without having my own. It helps to fill
a void. My other dear friend, Jill, having felt the loss of a failed

marriage and not having any children of her own, provided a common bond which evolved into a very beautiful friendship between us. I'm always surprised by how free it feels to be so bonded to others. I don't know that I was ready to open myself to such deep connections when I was younger. I don't know if I had the confidence to believe in lasting relationships. My parents' divorce shook me; it shook the very foundations of my beliefs. But in the end, I'm grateful for the experiences that allowed me to redefine my idea of family.

With Eric as my family now, I'm learning more about myself all the time. Every day we're helping each other to grow. I know what it is to have complete trust and loyalty. I have utter faith that this man I've chosen to join my life with will be by my side, no matter what. I know that there will be hard times, along with the good, but I now trust myself enough to know that nothing will break me. I can be who I am and still be cherished.

My parents both remarried over the years, and I remain extremely close to my mom and stepdad. I don't talk to my father much, nor to my brother and sister. Our family was divided over the past, and I don't know how the gulfs between us can ever really be bridged.

I still feel the pains of the past deeply, and my heart still aches when I hear a baby cry, or I face another Mother's Day with only my grief and sorrow for the children who will never be mine. But I recognize that it's okay to feel sad over the past, as long as we don't let it affect the present. Eric and I will probably continue to have four-legged children—dogs adopted from shelters—and be aunts and uncles to our friends' kids, and that's okay. It may be different from the norm or different than I imagined, but it's beautiful in its own way. Life is beautiful, each in its own way, just as you and I are.

23

Full Circle

I started the descent with a renewed strength and determination; I knew I was over halfway through the run. There were firefighters along the median, showing their support, and I ran by, giving them high-fives. They roared their approval, and the joy I felt with each bit of human kindness could have sustained me many miles. Perhaps that's how I lived my whole life, buoyed by the strength of others. And this, I finally realized, is the way we all should live: taking when we need to take and giving when we need to give. We all falter, and we all suffer, but we are never truly alone.

By the time we reached the bottom of the bridge, we'd run four and a half miles. I was tired, but I had to keep going. I hadn't stopped yet, and I didn't mean to now. We turned the corner at the end of the bridge, and I saw the crowds gathered along the sidewalks, cheering for the mass of runners. I knew there were only a few streets to turn down before we were done. Eric turned and saw the look on my face.

"Just remember being on the track," he said. "Keep going. You've got this, Betsy."

I focused on every step, every breath, just like I had at the beginning. I kept my eye on the next corner, one at a time. And then we turned the last corner and I could see the finish line at last. The roar of the crowd was deafening.

"Finish strong, Betsy."

I pumped my legs as hard as I could, closed my eyes, and left it all behind me. As I crossed the finish line, a wave of relief and gratitude washed over me, and I could not hold the tears in check. I had to keep walking, keep moving, or I'd collapse. Eric threw his arms around me, a newspaper reporter stuck a mic in my face, but nothing mattered except that I had done it.

After a while, we found a place to sit and recover. We hung out and took some pictures. I had met up with my prosthetist, Steven, who made this all possible with the running blade he had donated for me. We hugged each other with excitement and joy. Looking around, we could see friends, family, and strangers alike sharing in each other's triumph. We were all winners. No matter the physical differences among us, we were all winners. In the shade beneath a tree, we sat down to rehydrate and reflect on the past ninety minutes it took to run the 10K.

As the rush of adrenaline wore off and a quiet satisfaction overtook me, a woman passing by said, "You're an inspiration. Thank you. I saw you out there, and I knew I could do it too."

I looked at her—a stranger who was acknowledging this shared intimacy of inspiration—and I realized that it was mutual. I had inspired people, and they had inspired me. It was such a simple but profound notion in a world where we feel so singular in times of struggle. In that moment, I knew that I had truly come full circle in my life, to appreciate such a thing.

Giving up and giving in to despair is never an option. Don't let it be an option. There is so much to experience in life. I think back to my poster-child days with the March of Dimes, and I realize there are experiences in life that are meant to lift us up. But we'll never experience such things if we're too afraid to reach for them. If I can hold my own life up as anything, it's the ideal that nothing is perfect, but life must be lived. We just have to get out there and do it.

Betsy works as a registered nurse in adult critical care medicine and currently lives in Mount Pleasant, South Carolina. She also enjoys spending time with her golden collie rescue, gardening, star gazing and being in nature.

Made in the USA
Columbia, SC
27 July 2019